GLOBALIZATION AND COMMUNICATION POLICY IN INDIA

ABOUT THE AUTHORS

Dr. B.P. Mahesh Chandra Guru obtained Master's Degree in Mass Communication and Journalism (1980) and Ph.D. in Development Communication (1997). He has also worked as Journalist (Panchama), Research Associate (National Institute of Rural Development, Hyderabad), Assistant Director (Chandigarh), Lecturer (Bangalore University), Reader (Mangalore University) and Professor (University of Mysore) during the last three decades. He has also served the Karnataka Public Service Commission, Union Public Service Commission, University Grants Commission and National Assessment and Accreditation Council in different capacities. He has been a research consultant to some leading NGOs and media institutions in the country. He is presently heading the Department of Studies in Communication and Journalism, University of Mysore.

Dr. H.K. Mariswamy obtained Master's Degree in Mass Communication and Journalism (1980) and Ph.D. in Development Communication (1997). He has also worked as Journalist (Panchama), Lecturer (Karnatak University, Dharwad) and Associate Professor (Bangalore University) during the last three decades. He has also served the various universities across the country as member of Board of Studies and Board of Examiners. He has also adjudicated Ph.D. thesis as a subject experts. He has also successfully guided 10 research scholars. He is actively involved in progressive movements as a social activist and organizer. He is also a consultant to various media institutions and non-governmental organizations.

GLOBALIZATION AND COMMUNICATION POLICY IN INDIA

PROF. B.P. MAHESH CHANDRA GURU
and
PROF. H.K. MARISWAMY

CONCEPT PUBLISHING COMPANY PVT. LTD.
NEW DELHI-110059

ISBN-13 : 978-93-5125-103-3 (PB)

First Published 2014

Published and Printed by

Concept Publishing Company Pvt. Ltd.
A/15-16, Commercial Block, Mohan Garden
New Delhi-110059 (India)
T: 25351460, 25351794, *F*: 091-11-25357109
E: publishing@conceptpub.com, W: www.conceptpub.com
Editorial Office: H-13, Bali Nagar, New Delhi-110 015, India.

Cataloging in Publication Data—*Courtesy:* D.K. Agencies (P) Ltd. <docinfo@dkagencies.com>

Guru, B. P. Mahesh Chandra, 1957-
Globalization and communication policy in India / B.P. Mahesh Chandra Guru and H.K. Mariswamy.
p. cm.
Includes bibliographical references (p.) and index.
ISBN 9789351250685 (HB)
ISBN 9789351251033 (PB)

1. Communication policy—India. 2. Mass media and globalization. 3. Mass media and globalization—India. I. Mariswamy, H. K., joint author. II. Title.

DDC 302.20954 23

Dedicated to

Late Prof. Nadig Krishna Murthy
Doyen of Media Education in India

ಗುಲಬರ್ಗಾ ವಿಶ್ವವಿದ್ಯಾಲಯ

ಜ್ಞಾನಗಂಗಾ – ಗುಲಬರ್ಗಾ-585 106 – ಕರ್ನಾಟಕ
ದೂರವಾಣಿ : ಕ. 08472-263201 – 08472-263200
ನಿ. 08472-245065 – ಫ್ಯಾಕ್ಸ್ : 08472-263205
ಇ-ಮೇಲ್ : profetputtaiah@rediffmail.com - vcgug@rediffmail.com
ವೆಬ್ : www.gulbargauniversity.kar.nic.in

GULBARGA UNIVERSITY

"JNANA GANGA"
GULBARGA-585 106 - KARNATAKA - INDIA
Ph. : Off. 08472-263200 - 263201 - Resi. 245065 - Fax : 263205
Email : profetputtaiah@rediffmail.com - vcgug@rediffmail.com
web: www.gulbargauniversity.kar.nic.in

Prof. E. T. PUTTAIAH M.Sc.,Ph.D.
Vice-Chancellor

Foreword

In modern society, communication policy formulation assumes great significance since it provides sound ideological and operational norms and guidelines for the various stakeholders of media management. The public and private institutions formulate policies in order to achieve the goal of good governance. In a democracy, the media institutions constitute the fourth estate besides legislature, executive and judiciary. The media institutions have a social responsibility of functioning as informal university and opposition party outside the legislature. The media can also place facts, figures, ideas and guidelines with respect to several issues concerning public policy formulation from time-to-time.

The communication policy of a country is formally presented in the form of an official document which is ratified in the National Parliament. The communication policy decides the nature of media management and delivery of goods and services by the media institutions. Communication policy formulation is undertaken by the National Government in order to prevent the conflict of interest and safeguard public interest. In the age of globalization, media institutions are owned, managed and controlled by the market forces. In the present times media have become profit-centred industries rather than public service institutions. The media professionals have also become media executives rather than the representatives of people. The media are required to contribute towards promoting the just cause of the people struggling for freedom, independence and progress.

In the age of globalization of media, the world is becoming a much more integrated market based in capitalist or market place economics. Scholars have argued that effective legal measures should be designed and implemented to circumscribe the action of transnational corporations by requiring them to comply with specific criteria and conditions defined by national legislations which are formulated from time to time with due respect to local culture, environment and public interest. The phenomenon of media globalization along with the increasing abundance of media-text production has produced various effects which are being researched by communication scholars. The globalization has impacted the media services in India and abroad. The present work emphasizes that it is imperative to formulate a national policy on communication at this juncture in order to safeguard public interest.

Dr. B.P. Mahesh Chandra Guru and Dr. H.K. Mariswamy have served in different institutions and universities in different capacities. The present book '*Globalization and Communication Policy in India*' is indeed a welcome addition to the existing literature on media and globalization. I appreciate the efforts of both the scholars who have contributed significantly innovative ideas for the formulation national media policy in India in order to regulate the functions of both traditional and modern communications media and uphold professional ethics. I wish them the very best in all their academic endeavours.

Gulbarga
30th September, 2013

Prof. E.T. Puttaiah
Vice-Chancellor
Gulbarga University, Gulbarga

Preface

In a democracy, the media institutions constitute the fourth estate besides legislature, executive and judicial. Apart from government institutions, the educational institutions, social organizations, cultural organizations, non-governmental organizations and other agencies also exercise much influence over communication policy formulation. Communication policy formulation assumes profound significance in modern society since it enables the media organizations to follow the healthy practices and deliver the goods with due respect to democracy and public interest. Communication policy is also defined as a goal directed or purposive course of action followed by the media owners and professionals in an attempt to deal with public issues. Media organizations are required to function according to the constitutional guidelines, professional norms and social obligations. There are several stakeholders of communication policy formulation in modern society. The pressure groups also play a major role in sensitizing the policy makers and other stakeholders.

Globalization is driven by economic and technological changes. The process of globalization has affected the communications media institutions and operations decisively according to the empirical studies concerning the relationship between globalization and media. The driving force behind globalization is motivated by economic interests. The process of globalization concerns the relationship of globalization to neo-liberal economies. The present stage of globalization is re-described as Americanization. Practically, the new patterns of global communication are creating the new global cultural and economic orders which are strongly supported by global advertising and entertainment industry. The media technologies have developed fairly independently over a period of time. The phenomenon of media globalization along with the increasing abundance of media-text production has produced various effects which are noticed by the researchers. The global communication in the new millennium has brought about many effects which have blurred the cultural, political, economic, educational and technological boundaries.

The globalization of economy and media has posed series of challenges to the policy makers and professionals in India. A pluralistic and democratic country like India cannot have the luxury of free and irresponsible media. If the media institutions failed to regulate themselves in accordance with the constitutional obligations and norms of social responsibility, they have to be regulated by the government. The policy makers are responsible for evolving certain checks and balances in order to safeguard the local culture, environment, polity, economy, media and public interest. Hence, formulation of national communication policy at this juncture becomes highly imperative in India.

The book has five chapters. The first chapter deals with the fundamentals of communication. The 2nd chapter contains the basics of communication policy. The 3rd chapter involves the discussion on the relationship between globalization and world media. The 4th chapter presents the details about the impact of globalization on Indian media. The 5th chapter focuses the attention of scholars on communication policy formulation in India in the age of globalization. The last chapter of the book presents bibliographical details for the use of next generation of researchers and scholars. The book is the result of the authors' comprehensive evaluation of the impact of globalization on national media policy, system and operations in India. The book provides a good deal of analytical information on globalization and media policy in India. The book meets the objective of being a text book and reference book that provides relevant details pertaining to globalization and media policy to various stakeholders in India.

B.P. Mahesh Chandra Guru
H.K. Mariswamy

Acknowledgements

We express our profound sense of gratitude to our teachers Prof. H.S. Eshwara, Prof. K.V. Nagaraj and Prof. K. Puttaraju for their constant guidance and encouragement throughout our academic and professional career.

We are also indebted to Prof. V.G. Talwar, Former Vice-Chancellor, University of Mysore, Prof. K.S. Rangappa, present Vice-Chancellor, University of Mysore, Prof. B. Thimme Gowda, Vice-Chancellor, Bangalore University and Prof. E.T. Puttaiah, Vice-Chancellor, Gulbarga University for their kind encouragement and support.

We recall with gratitude our esteemed colleagues Prof. late B.A. Sridhara, Prof. A.S. Balasubramanya, Prof. N. Usha Rani, Prof. K.J. Joseph, Dr. B.K.Ravi, Dr. N. Sanjeevaraja, Dr. C.K. Puttaswamy, Dr. Sanjay Malagatti, Dr. Mahadevaswamy, Dr. M.S. Sapna and Dr. Kumaraswamy for their constant moral support.

We are highly indebted to the owner of Concept Publishing Company Pvt. Ltd., New Delhi for printing this book which fulfils the requirements of scholars, researchers, students and other stakeholders.

We also express my thanks to Mr. R. Gopala Krishna and M. Parashivamurthy for providing technical support towards making the book to its present form. Finally, we express our gratitude to the family members who have played a major role in making our career purposeful and rewarding.

B.P. Mahesh Chandra Guru
H.K. Mariswamy

Contents

1

Fundamentals of Communication

Introduction

Communication occupies an enviable status in the process of development. Communication creates awareness, opens up new vistas and facilitates development of individuals and organizations. The need for communication arises from the man's desire to express himself in a competitive environment in a meaningful manner. In this age of connectivity, communication cements all kinds of gaps, fosters togetherness, promotes better understanding and facilitates the development of the mankind in all spheres of human life. Communication has evolved over the years on the basis of expansion of human mind, development of technologies and application of technologies. All modern organizations use communication services to enlist the active participation of people in the process of development. In the age of globalization, communication plays a decisive role in bridging the communication gap and facilitating expansion of educational, social, economic, political and cultural activities across the globe. The world needs powerful communicators and facilitators of development. In this section, concept of communication, nature of communication, process of communication, types of communication, barriers to communication, essentials of communication, models of communication and impact of communication are mainly discussed.

Concept of Communication

The English word 'communication' has the Latin roots *communis* and *communicare,* meaning sharing of meaning and understanding based on friendship, mutual respect, equality and feeling of oneness. The closest Indian language equivalent to the original concept of communication is '*sadharanikaran*' which means human relationship building through meaningful dialogue or communication. The basis of human communication is nothing but the sharing of love and understanding which enrich the human life and culture. It rests on the fundamental principle that all human beings are essentially the same, fed by the same nature and nurtured by the same creator. But a mere sending of messages from the source to the receivers does not constitute the real communication. There should be sharing of ideas, meanings, thoughts, feelings and other sentiments which lead to coordinated actions.

Communication is as old as humanity itself. Communication has been viewed as the process of sharing information, experience and expertise between the source of communication and users of communication services. Communication is also defined as the exchange of information, education, entertainment, guidance, counselling and other services which benefit the mankind intellectually and otherwise. Scholars have considered communication as a relatively linear process of information transmission, causing or contributing to change in knowledge, attitudes and behaviours. Others view communication as a complex process which is closely associated with social, economic, political and cultural structures and processes.

Communication basically involves better human relationship building through social and cultural 'togetherness' according to several experts. It has several characteristics of an inter-disciplinary and multi-disciplinary social science. Communication studies are largely influenced by several institutional and social needs and rapid growth of the modern media of communication like press, film, radio, television, computer, satellites, telecommunication channels and so on. The discipline of communication had its roots in literary and linguistic studies carried out in Europe and American continents.

Scholars have offered some definitions which reveal the facets of communication and facilitated an understanding of the concept of communication.

Revesz states: "Communication encompasses all forms of expression which serve the purpose of mutual understanding."

Berelson and Steiner observe: "Communication is the transmission of information, ideas, emotions, skills, etc. by the use of symbols, words, pictures, figures, graphs, etc. It is the act or process of transformation that is usually called communication."

Anderson notes: "Communication is the process by which we understand others and in turn endeavour to be understood by them. It is dynamic, constantly changing and shifting in response to the total situation."

Ruesch comments: "Communication is the process that links discontinuous parts of the living world to one another."

Schacter writes: "Communication is the means by which power is exerted."

According to Newman and Summer, "Communication is an exchange of facts, ideas, opinions or emotions by two or more persons. Communication is also defined as intercourse by words, letters, symbols or messages and as a way that one organization member shares meaning and understanding with another."

Leyland Brown considers communication as the transmission and interchange of facts, ideas, feelings or course of action.

Charles E. Redfield perceives: "Communication is the broad field of human interchange of facts and opinions and not the technologies of telephone, telegraph, radio and the like."

Allen Louis points out that "Communication is the sum of all the things one person thus when he wants to create understanding in the mind of another. It involves a systematic and continuous process of telling, listening and understanding."

Ordway Tead narrates: "Communication is a composite of information given and received, of a learning experience in which certain attitudes, knowledge and skills exchange, carrying with them alterations of behaviour, of listening effort by all involved, of a sympathetic fresh examination of issues by the communicator himself, of a sensitive interaction of points of view leading to a higher level of shared understanding and common intention."

UNESCO documents: "Communication maintains and animates life. It creates a common pool of ideas, strengthens the feeling of togetherness through exchange of messages and translates thought into action."

Montagu and Matson (2008) describe the fact of communication thus: "Communication is a fact in the world of human beings, animals and plants, and is an ever continuing process going on all the time. It is as necessary to human, animal and vegetable existence as life itself. The need for communication is as basic as the hunger for food and drink, perhaps even more so. Communication is the name we give to the countless ways that humans have of keeping in touch—not just words and music, pictures and print, nods and becks, postures and plumages; to every move that catches someone's eye and every sound that resonates upon another's Year."

All these scholars have commonly emphasized that communication is the life blood of individuals, organizations, governments and societies. Effective communication is very essential to achieve success either at individual level or at institutional level. Every individual has to constantly interact with his/her fellow beings through meaningful communication. Communication facilitates better establishment of human relationships and network development which matter most in the lives of the people. The need for communication arises from the man's desire to grow further and achieve progress by enlisting active cooperation and support from the fellow citizens.

Nature of Communication

The art and craft of communication have evolved over the years all over the world. The journey of communication has several stages, namely—sounds, grunts, actions, gestures, gesticulations, spoken word, written word, folk theatre forms, newspapers, magazines, cinema, radio, television, telecommunication, satellite communication, information and communication technologies, social media and so on. In the present times, the mankind is blessed with traditional media, new media and multi-media campaigns and transactions which have brought about interactive communication across the globe.

The communication encompasses wide areas and actions involving several stakeholders, media, technologies and actions. The communication becomes complete and effective only when the receivers correctly comprehend the message and purpose of communication and act upon it as envisaged by the source of communication. Communication sustains the growth and development of individuals and institutions. There must be two parties in the process of communication, namely—sender and receiver. The nature of communication is exchange of messages and interaction between these two parties.

Communication becomes effective when the message is shared and understood by both the parties. There can be no communication if the information is not properly understood by the receiver in the same sense as it was intended to be by the communicator. The receiver need not agree or accept the information, idea, opinion etc. put forward by the sender. It is sufficient if the information is understood even though it is not accepted by the receiver.

The scope of communication is very wide and comprehensive by nature. It is known for unlimited dimensions and purposes. It is a continuous process of exchange of facts, ideas, feelings, opinions and interactions with others. Communication involves several tools, technologies and contents which are multi-faceted by nature. The basic elements of communication include—message, sender, encoding, channel, receiver, decoding and response. The feedback enables the communicator to carry out corrections in accordance with the felt needs of the receiver.

Beltron (1978) elaborates the need for communication thus: "A human being's need for communication is as strong and as basic as the need to eat, sleep and love. It is both an individual and a social need. It is both a natural individual demand and a requirement of social existence to use communication resources in order to engage in the sharing of experiences, through symbol-mediated interaction."

Oral communication facilitates understanding between the source of communication and users of communication through the language while non-verbal communication conveys the message through signs, symbols and gestures. Oral communication reaches out to the limited number of users while non-verbal communication reaches out to plenty of users with a difference. It is highly significant because it conveys meaning to others without the help of words.

Burgoon (1994) highlights the intricacies of non-verbal communication thus: "Just as a coding system must have semantic and syntactic rules, so must non-verbal signals as they are combined to form messages if they are to be treated as a coding system. This assumption delimits the non-verbal domain to the extent that it excludes behaviours which lack consistent meanings and behaviours that fail to be combined in systematic, grammatical ways with other non-verbal signals.

The nature of communication is mainly dependent on the structure of a particular society. Communication in such a society will negate the very meaning of communication. There are broadly five varieties of communication—intrapersonal communication (taking place within an individual), interpersonal communication (between individuals and groups), group communication (within members of a particular group), organizational communication (within employers and employees of an organization) and mass communication (within society or nation). However, mass communication has gained tremendous significance because of mass media which reach out to the millions of people all over the world.

Scholars have identified the distinction between communication and mass communication. Communication really brings about mutual understanding while mass communication simply includes the dissemination of information or ideas without any mutual understanding between the two parties (source and receivers). The mass media like newspapers, magazines, film, radio and television have the capacity to provide the benefits of information, education and entertainment to countless number of people who are spread across the length and breadth of the society from local to global.

Communication basically involves active interaction with physical, biological and social environments. The people are required to adapt themselves to the changing environment by following right communication norms and channels. Verbal and non-verbal communications are required to enable the people to share experiences and expertise in the society. The human beings are required to communicate with others regardless of the languages and forms of communication. Ricardo C. Noseda distinguishes between communication and information thus: "Communication is not an act but a process by which an individuality enters into mental cooperation with another individuality until they come to constitute a common conscience."

Process of Communication

Denis McQuail (1975) defines: "Communication is a process which increases commonality—but also requires elements of commonality for it to occur at all." The act of communication becomes a futile exercise if the commonality is not established between the sender and receiver. A common language and tools of communication facilitate a sense of commonality and community." The scholar sees human communication in linear terms as the sending of meaningful messages from one person to another. Communication is not an act of sending discreet messages back and forth, but a process of mutual participation in a society which consists of members who share a common culture.

Communication etymologically implies sharing a community of interests and social cohesion based on social needs and aspirations. The MacBride Commission (1980) states: "Communication maintains and animates life. It is also the motor and expression of social activity and civilization. The task of communication has become ever more complicated and subtle to contribute to the liberation of mankind from want, oppression and fear and to unite it in community and communion, solidarity and understanding. However, unless some basic structural changes are introduced, the potential benefits of technological and communication development will hardly be put at the disposal of the majority of mankind."

The process of communication is two-fold. The first phase involves the encoding of message by the sender and transmission of the message to the receiver. In the second phase the receiver decodes the message in accordance with his own education, experience and ability, encodes it and formulates it in the form of a response. The process of communication becomes complete when this message reaches the original communicator or source and he decodes it in accordance with his own frame of reference. All the five senses play an important role in times of reception of the message which is the life blood of communication. The manner and mode of receiving a transmitted message is then contingent upon which of the senses is predominantly active at that moment. Basically, all communication activities are goal oriented and serve specific purposes. The sender and receiver must be aware of the goal of communication in order to facilitate better understanding of the messages. The convergence of the goals of the sender and receiver really makes the process of communication effective.

David K. Berlo has noted the six steps involved in the process of communication such as—ideation, encoding, transmission, receiving, decoding and acting. The message includes the subject matter of communication. The transmitter is a person who communicates a message. The process of conversion of subject matter into symbols is called as encoding. The traditional and modern channels of communication are used for the purpose of transmission of information. The receiver is the person to whom the message is directed. The decoding is the process of translation of an encoded message into ordinary understandable language. The acting involves the eliciting of an intended response from the receivers of communication. The feedback enables the communicator to carry out certain corrections or to make certain modifications either in the message formulation or in the act of communication.

Communication is a process that involves several distinct phases. Basically communication process involves stimulus and response. The stimulus arises from the communicator (source of communication) and the receiver responds to the communication. The process of communication does not become complete if the receiver fails to understand the message communicated by the source. The process of communication begins with a purpose. The source of communication delivers the message with a purpose. The communicator has to encode the idea or message which gets a communicable form. Encoding involves choosing the right language symbols, contents and devices for the purpose of making communication quite clear. The communicator has to choose appropriate channels which fit into the context, receivers and environment of communication. The transmission becomes complete when the message reaches the receivers through certain channels. The receivers are required to decode the message and understand the point of view of the communicator. The communication becomes complete only when the receivers understand the message and act upon them as envisaged by the communicator. Thus, the process of communication involves several steps under the normal circumstances.

Basically every act of communication is the process of interaction. Lasswell has explained the process of communication thus: "who says what through what channel to whom and with what effect". The process of communication basically includes five major elements, namely—source, message, channel, receiver and effect. The source is a very important element of communication because all the messages usually emanate from the source. The source should be invariably knowledgeable, experienced, specialized and competent enough to serve the purpose of communication through utmost clarity of thought and action. There are individual sources and institutional sources. Parents, teachers, opinion leaders, community leaders, resource persons, change agents, catalysts of development, organizers and others usually constitute the individual sources. The government organizations, political parties, educational institutions, research organizations, development institutions, political parties, cultural organizations and other non-government organizations usually constitute the institutional sources. Modern institutions are required to reach out to various constituent publics who matter most from the point of view organizational development in the present times. Modern organizations are also required to enter into the good books of various stakeholders and enlist their active participation in the management and development of organizations. Organizations should also educate the various stakeholders about the policies, priorities, agenda, operations, goods, services and so on in order to gain public acceptance in the modern society. Hence, organizations are required to communicate constantly, consistently and effectively with various publics who are their angel guardians in the present times.

The message constitutes the next important element of communication process. The message is the life blood of communication. It should be fully and properly understood by the people. The message should be formulated by the creative writers in order to make it simple, direct, specific, understandable and effective. The source of communication should identify better content producers and enable the audience to understand the messages and respond positively to the source of communication. As far as possible, local idioms, jargons, phrases and other contents should be used to make the messages quite alive, active and understandable.

The source of communication usually makes use of several

communication channels which fit into a given context. Inter-personal, traditional, modern, advanced, outdoor, new media, social network sites and other channels are used by the source in order to bridge the communication gap between the source of communication and users of communication. The source should consciously choose the channels which are simple, accessible, credible, effective and useful to the receivers under the normal circumstances. Media selection is indeed a scientific exercise which is carried out on the basis of authentic data in modern society. There are experts in media selection who play a major role in the selection of media which suit the convenience of the receivers of communication.

The receivers of communication should be suitably informed, educated, organized, motivated and directed in order to accept certain points of view and respond to the needs of the source of communication. The demographic features of the receivers of communication should be properly understood by the source in order to make communication user friendly, need based and utility oriented. The source of communication should also have a thorough knowledge about the receivers and provide tailor-made communication to the receivers in order to enhance the utility of the messages. Hence, receivers-friendly communication serves a good purpose.

The source of communication should also make use of the experts in the conduction of the evaluation of the effectiveness of the messages put across by them through various channels. The effects of communication should be constantly measured in order to make suitable changes and modifications in the process of communication. The source should also feel the pulse of the receivers and make necessary corrections to the approaches of the communication. Hence, scientific and systematic evaluation of the effects of communication facilitates purification, perfection and standardization of communication services in the present age of competitiveness.

In the process of communication, the various components discharge their functions according to their basic acculturation. Most theorists agree that communication has three shades of meaning—exchange of information verbally, non-verbally and both for the purpose of establishing mutual understanding and cooperation. The source of communication should understand that receivers are not passive but dynamic forces who can decide the fate of communications media.

The source of communication, message of communication, channels of communication, receivers of communication and effects of communication should be properly understood by the individuals and organizations in the present times. Every element in the process of communication is equally important. The communication services should be delivered on the basis of authentic data, proper planning and perfect strategies in order to gain maximum benefits. Communication is power and it should be used for the purpose of creating awareness among the receivers about the various nation building, problem solving and other activities in modern society.

George Gerbner (1985) refers to the process of mass communication which discharge massive symbol systems into the mainstream of common consciousness thus: "Mass communication is carried on through messages that the largely mass produced and/or distributed by complex industrial structures. The members of a public born in a particular cultural context select and interpret messages in a certain way. Their selection and interpretation depends on the system of messages that regulate social relationships. Such cultivation and public acculturation is carried on through the massively mediated messages which over a long period of time provide a functional perspective of *existence* (what is), *priority* (what is important), *values* (what is right and wrong) and *relationships* (what is related to what)."

Vilanilam (2005) defines communication as the exchange of information between and among human beings for the promotion of mutual and common understanding and desirable social action. Communication takes place in society at various levels ranging from individual to mass society. The pyramid of communication has its base at the intrapersonal segment. Mass communication occupies only the apex of the pyramid. The world 'mass' means common people who are countless in number. The phrase 'mass communication' indicates the flow of information and communication to the large number of the people in which one's individuality is lost.

McQuail explains the concept of mass by using four important aspects, namely—large aggregate, undifferentiated, mainly negative image and lacking order. Scholars have provided a new dimension to mass communication which basically involves sharing of information and communication between the mass media and people. Mass media are the means of communication which facilitate transmission of messages to large, heterogeneous, and anonymous masses of people living in different regions of a locality, nation or the world. Print media (newspapers, magazines, etc.), electronic media (radio, television, film, etc.) and new media (Internet, E-mail, etc.) are duly considered as mass media since they cater to the needs of millions of users.

Shanon and Weaver conceived of communication as a system composed of five essential parts plus noise, namely—an information source, a transmitter, a channel, the receiver and the destination. Wilbur Shramm adapted Shanon and Weaver's model to human communication but stressed on encoding and decoding aspects which are crucial in the process of communication. He defines: 'Communication is the sharing of information, ideas and attitudes". He endorsed the Aristotelian principle that communication always requires at least three elements—source, message and destination.

O.J. Harris suggested certain ideas which could be considered by the source of communication in order to facilitate meaningful sharing of ideas between the two parties. They include :

- The sender should attempt to remove biases and tensions that may cloud his own mind.
- Before communicating, the communicator should attempt to determine what the real need for communication is.
- It is desirable to learn as much about the receiver as possible before communicating with him.
- In issuing the message, it is important to have the receiver's attention so that he will be sensitive to what is being sent to him.
- The sender should communicate as directly with the intended receiver as is practical.
- The use of symbols (words, gestures, etc.) that are simple and uncomplicated is helpful.
- Repetition of messages may be helpful in conveying the intended thoughts.
- Also desirable is consistency in actions and in communication of thoughts.
- Messages should be timed so that they are received when they are needed and are not misconducted as a result of other thoughts on the receiver's mind.

Types of Communication

Intra-personal communication takes place within an individual in the form of reflection, contemplation, meditation, introspection and so on. The people are bound to rely upon intra-personal communication from birth to death. Inter-personal communication is direct face-to-face communication which takes place between two or more persons it is more common, influential and persuasive form of communication that benefits both the parties. Group communication takes place between the leader of the group and followers. It provides opportunities to seek information on any subject and facilitates participatory communication. Organizational communication occurs between the management and employees and organization and various stakeholders, namely—investors, suppliers, distributors, consumers, media professionals, government officials, members of the local community and so on. Mass communication takes place between the modern mass media and society. It is also known as massive communication which involves big media and countless number of receivers.

Mass communication basically answers to the fundamental questions—who says what, in which channel, to whom and with what effect according to Harold D. Laswell. The scholar identified three prominent functions of communication namely—surveillance of the environment, correlation of components of society, and cultural transmission between generations.

There are several methods and channels of communication. Prominent among them include—oral communication, written communication, non-verbal communication, visual communication and so on.

The oral communication refers to the spoken word which takes the form of sounds and words. The development of vocabulary and languages has enriched the process of oral communication. It plays a major role in the lives of people and organizations. Oral communication is primarily based on direct person to person communication which is a two-way communication. The spoken words carry considerable weightage regardless of time and space. It works well in case of a small and compact group. But, oral communication is also reflected in the form of talks, speeches, meetings, discussions, seminars, conferences and other occasions through active use of microphone, loudspeaker, amplifiers, tape recorders, telephone, radio, television and so on. The oral communication is extremely beneficial while dealing with the masses in any organization or society.

The written communication is also a powerful method of communication. After experimenting with writing on sand, stone, leaves etc., man invented paper, pen, books and other print media. Newspapers, magazines, professional journals, books and other print media are effective tools of mass communication. Written communication is known for permanence, credibility, documentation and other advantages. The communication skills, vocabulary and art of writing make written communication forceful and effective. The written communication takes time to reach out to the target groups when compared to oral communication. However, the invention of telephone, telex, fax, e-mail and other devices has reduced the time involved in message transmission. The written communication is less interactive when compared to oral communication.

The non-verbal communication is neither oral nor written by nature. The oral communication is based on listening while the written communication is based on reading. But, the non-verbal communication refers to the type of communication that does not use words. It is primarily based on observation. The body language, gestures, postures, appearance, personal space, timing, codes, signals, facial expression and other personal qualities have enriched the process of non-verbal communication. The non-verbal communication assumes great relevance in direct contact, face to face communication and interactions. The non-verbal communication primarily communicates the messages to the target group through conscious gestures, postures and body language. The receivers should be in a position to clearly see the face, gesture, posture, dress, appearance, voice, tone, pitch, pace, intensity and other elements of non-verbal communication. Studies have revealed that non-verbal communication has an overwhelming impact on the audience. The oral or verbal communication can supplement and compliment the non-verbal communication if used appropriately.

The visual communication is practiced through pictures, graphs, charts, symbols, signs and other channels. The signs, symbols, pictures, films, transparencies, floppies, projectors and other channels are very effective channels of visual communication. The audio-visual communication has emerged as the most sophisticated method of communication over a period of time. It basically involves demonstration and presentations through various audio-visual aids. The audio-visual communication is basically skill oriented. They are quite useful in facilitating interactive learning and communication. The use of multi-media presentations has gained immense popularity in the modern world.

The upward communication usually moves upwards, namely from bottom to top levels in the organizational hierarchy. It enables the top management to understand the problems, needs and demands of the people at the grassroots level either in an organization or a society. In a democracy, the people have a right to communication. They are free to air their grievances and register their protest as and when required.

The downward communication moves from top to bottom. It also occurs from high command to the people and from top management to the employees. The top level authorities communicate certain things in order to make people understand the policies, programmes, activities, contributions and through orders, letters, memos and other channels. The top level authorities are also required to take note of the problems of the people or employees and facilitate better feedback collection, analyses and remedial measures.

The formal communication takes place through formal systems and opportunities. Staff meetings, union-management meetings, conferences, review meetings, customer meets and other occasions are used by the organizational leaders for the purpose of establishing rapport with the masses or employees.

The informal communication takes place in an unstructured manner and outside the formal fora. The informal communication is based on simplicity, flexibility, spontaneity and other values of communication. It is more convenient method of communication in a small community or organizations. It cuts across hierarchical differences and barriers.

The lateral communication is neither upward nor downward. It proceeds in the horizontal manner and takes place among the equals. It is also a more democratic means of communication which facilitates better interaction between the organizers and beneficiaries. There are several interactive communication channels in modern society as well as organizations. Prominent among them include meetings, conferences, tele conferences, multi media presentations and so on. These various types of communication are found in modern organizations and societies. Each type of communication has its own advantages and limitations. But participatory communication is known as the best type of communication in the world since it facilitates better interaction, understanding and cooperation between the source of communication and beneficiaries of communication.

Barriers to Communication

The process of communication is bound to create certain barriers if the source of communication and receivers of communication fail to achieve commonality of understanding. The source of communication should be conscious of the background of the receivers, needs of the receivers, expectations of the receivers and other aspects of receivers. The receivers should also understand the intentions of the source, efforts of the source, strategies of the source and other aspects of source of communication. In the process of communication, certain precautions are required to prevent communication gaps between the sender and receiver. These barriers hamper the communication and create misunderstanding, non-cooperation, adversity and other complexities.

Scholars have also identified the barriers to communication which include—physical barriers, psychological barriers, and mechanical barriers. The physical distance between the sender and receiver also causes communication barrier. Both the parties should be physically brought together in order to understand each other and share the ideas, experience and expertise which are disseminated or transmitted in an act of communication. The attitude, mindset, behavioural patterns and other psychological barriers are also found in the process of communication. The sender and receiver should enjoy the benefit of like-mindedness in order to come together, share each others perspectives and achieve a cooperative communication endeavour. The communication channels should also be used in proper combinations. The non-availability of power, equipments and other communicative devices also constitute the mechanical barriers to communication.

The physical barriers include—the competing stimulus, environmental stress, subjective stress and ignorance of the medium. The sender and receiver of communication should achieve a highly cooperative communication environment in order to facilitate better understanding. The presence of competing stimulus mars the process of communication. The sender and receiver should have a friendly, flexible and democratic communication environment in order to share the knowledge and experience. The environmental stress produces major threat to communication and creates communication gaps between the sender and receiver. The subjective stress should also be overcome in order to facilitate flow of ideas and experiences. The receivers should be aware of the features of the medium of communication. They must be able to understand the basic features of traditional and modern channels of communication and gain absolute familiarity with the medium of communication. Otherwise, the receivers might mistake the medium or message in the process of communication.

Asha Kaul (2002) enumerates the barriers to communication which need to be identified and overcome in order to make the process of communication complete and purposeful. She has listed the prominent barriers to communication which include loss in impact, ineffective grasp of messages, dichotomy in reception and comprehension, partial grasp of topic, distancing from the speaker, lack of interest, mental turbulence, misunderstanding, grouping for the right message, biased listening, lack of collaborative effort, mental block, absence of feedback and so on.

The scholar has also suggested certain cardinal rules for overcoming communication barriers which include proper communication planning, clarification of ideas, creation of a climate of trust and confidence, time management, reinforcement of words with actions, effective communication, clarity in messages, purposeful communication, use of simple language, persuasive communication and so on. The communication source is primarily responsible for the prevention of the barriers to communication. The receivers of communication are also required to develop a favourable mindset and grasp the essentials of communication with lot of interest and enthusiasm.

Essentials of Communication

Scholars have also identified the functions and dysfunctions of mass communication since the consequences of communication are both manifest and latent in reality. In fact, every function can also become a dysfunction in certain situation. According to Wright (1959), the consumer of predigested ideas, opinions and views becomes an ineffectual citizen, less capable of functioning as a rational man. The process of mass communication becomes effective if the means of communication enable the large groups of people in different locations to receive the same information in the same language. In this context, 'large' means immensely large, to be counted in the millions rather than in the thousands in a given circumstance.

The role of communications media is well appreciated and documented by various scholars at different times. Walter Lippmann (1922) once said: "Every newspaper when it reaches the reader is the result of a series of selections as to what items shall be printed, in what position they will be printed, how much space each shall occupy, what emphasis each shall have. There are no objective standards here. There are conventions." The observations made by Lippmann primarily deals with the delivery of media services on the basis of established conventions and practices rather than professional ethics and considerations.

The objectives of communication are many and varied. There are several types of communication which are practiced in the modern society. The significance of communication is seldom questioned by anybody in this world at any time. Communication is an all time necessity. Creative, effective and purposeful communication always matters in the world. Peter Drucker states: "Your effectiveness depends on your ability to reach others through the spoken or written word." The individuals and institutions are required to make their presence felt mainly through effective communication. The individuals and organizations can cut across all the barriers to communication and achieve remarkable success in establishing and sustaining mutually beneficial relationship with other stakeholders of development.

Communication scholars have discussed the essentials of communication in their speeches and writings adequately. They have emphatically stated that there is no substitute for effective communication which is the driving force of development individually and collectively. Communication is a planned, deliberate and systematic exercise which demands complete understanding of essentials of good communication among the various practitioners. They are as follows:

Clarity of Thought

The communicators should have absolute clarity of thoughts and deeds. Every communication should be goal-oriented. The communicators should be clear about what they should achieve through the process of communication. A clear cut communication perspective has to be developed in order to prepare grounds for effective dissemination of information to the target group. Mobilization of the resources, ideas and actions is very essential for the accomplishment of the tasks of communication in this age of competitiveness.

Understanding the Mission

The communicators should understand the nature, scope, significance and methods of delivering need based communication to the target group. They must know how to live up to the expectations of the target group in competitive business and media environments. They must collect relevant information, consolidate the information and correlate the information in order to prepare a blueprint for designing and implementing communication services which would satisfy the needs of the target group. They must also consult the experts, veterans and other resource persons and grasp the essentials of the mission in the right spirit. The communication should not be perceived as a casual exercise. It should be perceived as a mission which benefits the organizations and society. The communicators should also assume the role of missionaries in order to achieve optimum success in their mission.

Assessment of the Needs

The communicators should be aware of the needs and demands of the target group. They must design and deliver the communication services in accordance with the felt needs of the target group and ground realities. They must also develop the profile of the target group, understand the media access, examine the affordability of the audience, examine the cost-benefit ratio and workout a practically feasible media strategy. The media should be accessible to the target group and the message should reach out to the target group in order to enhance the status of communication.

Content Development

The communicators should consult the subject specialists and creative writers in order to produce subject-specific, target group specific, mission-specific and utility oriented script which would fit into the context of media and environment. General messages should be replaced by specific messages. Complex messages should be replaced by simple messages. Scholarly messages should be replaced by the user friendly messages. In reality, the messages should be produced with lot of caution and responsibility in order to avoid ambiguity and inconvenience to the users. The contents should be free from unhealthy, objectionable and contemptuous messages in order to prevent harmful contents and penal actions. The communicators should ensure that the message reaches the receivers in a language which is highly creative, simple and understandable.

Media Selection

The communicators should also know that all communications media are not equally capable of delivering goods and doing justice to their role as effective channels of communications. The media which fit into the context, culture, environment, audience and mission should be identified and utilized by the communicators. Hence, the communicators should make use of the services of experts in order to select an ideal medium or ideal media mix for the communication of messages which would benefit the target group.

Communication Strategies

The communicators should understand the process of communication and find out the best strategies which would bridge the communication gap between the communicators and target group. In this age of competitive communication, the communicators should appreciate the various steps involved in communication in terms of message formulation, media selection, encoding, decoding, transmission, comprehension, feedback analysis and so on. It is necessary to wipe out the communication barriers and enhance the status of communication through adoption of practically viable communication strategies.

Training and Orientation

The communicators are not born, they are made. The organizers of communication campaigns should understand the need and importance of trained, skilled and competent communicators in order to achieve optimum utilization of the resources, time, opportunities and so on. The target group wishes to get the best possible and most effective communication services from the source of communication. Hence, the organizers should identify the talent, mobilize the talent, train the human resources, upgrade the communication skill and achieve maximum success.

Planned Communication

The communicators cannot achieve commendable success on the basis of rough work and guess work. Inappropriate, inadequate and inefficient planning would create more communication barriers and failures. They must collect authentic information about the place of communication, context of communication, target group, media selection, message formulation, designing the strategies, implementing the communication programmes and other aspects of the process of communication. They must also evaluate the feasibility of the communication project and develop appropriate strategies in order to successfully reach out to the people, convey the message, enhance greater understanding, collect feedback and improve the state of affairs. Hence, the communicators should plan their programmes in consultation with the experts and in depth understanding of ground realities.

Delivery of Goods

The communicators should be aware of their mission, target group, methods of delivery of service and other aspects of communication. They should have the right perspective about the communication mission and deliver the goods. The delivery of communication services should be on the basis of proper assessment of the ground realities and evaluation of the strengths and weaknesses of communication. They must be very clear about the advantages and disadvantages of the methods of communication and deliver the goods which would fulfil the aspirations of the target group.

Cost Consciousness

The communicators should be aware of the cost-benefit ratio with reference to the delivery of communication services. They must know how to ensure the optimum utilization of available resources and prevent wasteful expenditure as far as possible. They must understand the direct and indirect costs in the delivery of communication services including media management and message formulation. They should work out the costs in consultation with the specialists in budgeting and media management. The results achieved by the process of communication should justify the costs involved in the project. The communicators should make conscious efforts to make their communication system and operation cost effective.

Time Management

The communicators should understand the value of time management with reference to delivery of goods and services in the name of communication. They must implement the communication project without giving any scope for delay, wasteful expenditure and unnecessary activities. They must have a meaningful time table for the production of media services and delivery of media services in order to prevent waste of time and resources. They must understand the speedy, efficient and timely delivery of goods and services which would facilitate the completion of the project within the allotted deadline. The communicators should have time consciousness and achieve success with respect to delivery of goods well in time.

Optimum Utilization of Opportunity

The communicators should know how to develop a positive approach and ensure optimum utilization of the opportunities. Good planning and execution of the communication services are required to ensure optimum utilization of opportunities. The communicators should develop the right mental attitude, race against the time and rise to the occasion in order to build image for their organization, enhance the reputation their organization and satisfy the target group. They should take the responsibility for making optimum utilization of time, resources, manpower, energy and opportunity.

Feedback Collection and Analysis

The communicators should attach great importance to the collection of feedback from the target group who always matter most. They must collect feedback from the receivers and find out where they stand professionally and otherwise. They must feel the pulse of the target group, understand their limitations, find out better methods of delivery of goods and improve the quality of communication services on the basis of scientific feedback collection and analysis. Communication is basically a two-way approach which should enable the service providers and beneficiaries to understand each other. The beneficiaries have a right to air their views, disagree with the communicators and demand better delivery of messages in a democratic environment. Hence, the organizers should correct their mistakes, enrich their initiatives and improve the delivery system on the basis of scientific evaluation.

Improving the Delivery System

The communicators should make conscious efforts to improve their perception, communication skills, organizational competence, media selection, message formulation, delivery of communication services and other aspects. Conscious, constant and consistent efforts are required to improve the quality of communication services and status of communication management. They should perceive that there is no substitute for quality of communication services. They must also take other stakeholders of communication into confidence and design the communication strategies in consultation with the experts. They should understand that these factors bring in a new dimension to the entire process of communication. Effective communication becomes more challenging task that lies ahead of the communicators.

Models of Communication

Communication is an art and science. It is a fundamental activity which is as old as the mankind is. Communication facilitates better interaction between individual and individuals, individuals and groups, groups and organizations, organizations and governments and governments and societies. As a matter of fact no individual can live in an island. Isolation brings about annihilation and integration brings about the prosperity of the individuals. Modern organizations cannot achieve any success in the absence of planned, deliberate and systematic communication which bridges the communication gap. There are several models of communication which are designed by various philosophers and experts over a period of time.

Aristotle gave the first model of communication which had sender, receiver and message as principal components. He proposed a simplistic model of communication and emphasized the persuasive tactics used by the senders of communication. In his model the source or sender was of primary importance. The process of communication was one-way.

Lasswell extended the scope of Aristotle's model of communication by laying emphasis on the channel which the source of communication used for the purpose of communicating certain things and obtaining favourable responses from the receivers. He laid emphasis on speaker, message and channel. His model also consisted of a one-way direction of communication.

Shanon-Weaver integrated the concepts proposed in the earlier models of communication and emphasized the importance of the encoding process prior to the transmission of the message. This model primarily recognized the importance of the sign theory which stated that the message should never be imparted in its raw form. He stated that the message should always be encoded in a form which would be accepted by the receiver. They also recognized the potential of noise in distorting the message. The model highlighted one-way direction of communication with a feedback. It was a major step since it emphasized the move to a two-way process of communication.

Wilber Schramm presented three models of communication-each an improvement on the existing one. The first model was in tune with the model of Shanon-Weaver and laid emphasis on the encoding phase in the process of communication. But Schramm did not attach any importance to the element of noise and restricted himself only to the source of communication. The direction of the flow of communication was indeed one-way. In his second model, Schramm extended the scope of his theory by highlighting the need for sharing the experience between the source of communication and receivers of communication. He identified two important elements of communication, namely—sender and receiver. He also stressed that the message should be encoded in a form which was acceptable to the receiver. The receiver was primarily taken into consideration by Schramm even though the second model was one-way. The third model of communication proposed by Schramm is considered as a major breakthrough in the field of communication by the scholars. The third model highlighted the significance of a response from the receiver. It pointed out that the receiver after decoding the message should transmit the response to the sender. This model focused the attention of the communication scholars on feedback system which is the basis for the improvement of the quality of communication.

Katz-Lazarsfeld proposed a model which was related to mass communication. According to this model, the sender encoded a message and transmitted information through mass media to an opinion leader who finally disseminated it to the masses. They identified four major elements of communication, namely—sender, receiver, message and opinion leader. The direction of communication was also one-way.

Westley-MacLean proceeded one step ahead of Katz and Lazarsfeld and provided a communication model which laid emphasis on interpersonal communication. They suggested that there should be a sender who would selectively encode the message to be transmitted to the receiver. The receiver would decode it after receiving it and then encode it either to the original sender or to other individuals in a modified form. They laid emphasis on sender, receiver and feedback. The direction of communication was circular with an inbuilt feedback system.

Berlo proposed another communication model based on the skills and experience of the source of the communication. He suggested that the sender encodes the message and transmits the same through one of the five senses. The reception of the message depends upon the receiver and his understanding of the message in a given context. He was the first scholar who emphasized the role of perception in the reception of message. He observed that communication gap occurred on account of discrepancy in the understanding of the messages. The four major components of his model were the source, the receiver, the meaning and the process. Berlo suggested a communication model which was only one-way.

Newcomb presented a communication model which was primarily based on the reaction of individuals to each other. This model was based on the recognition of the importance of harmon and consistency in any act of communication. Newcomb identified two important elements of communication, namely receiver and meaning. The flow of communication as suggested by Newcomb was triangular.

Dance suggested another communication model which emphasized that encoding the decoding of the messages in the process of communication is dependent on the previous communication experience of the receivers. He highlighted the importance of communication with special reference to encoding and decoding the message. This model observed a helical-spiral path.

Watlawick-Beavin-Jackobson proposed that the exchange of information, ideas and experiences in any kind of communication was primarily dependent on the behaviour of the interact ants. The scholars stressed that the communicative experience primarily depended on the relationship between the individuals and varied from one individual to another. They introduced a new element of meta communication in which receiver, meaning and outcome of communication were interrelated. They were the first scholars who clearly stated that communication is a two-way process.

Rogers-Kincaid suggested that individuals needed to be linked to one another through networks and operations. They identified the individuals who needed to be linked through social networks, information resources and time management. The direction of communication observed by this model was spiral. All these models have commonly identified sender, channel, content, receiver and effects. The sender and receiver are required to understand each other, share each others experience and proceed in one direction in order to in make communication a mutually beneficial exercise. The discrepancies are bound to occur if the sender and receiver deviate from rule-based communication under normal circumstances.

Some scholars have also formulated Speech Act Theory which highlights the rule-governed behaviour of the sender and receiver. The theory reflected a definite shift in the meaning according to a change in the context or situation. The scholars insisted that the sender and receiver should conform to certain rule-based behaviour, etiquettes and norms of communication which have three major dimensions. They include—(a) knowledge of the sender of the rules of communication, (b) the recipient's conformity to the rules, and (c) the extent to which the recipient either conforms or deviates in a particular context willingly or unwillingly.

Some ethno methodologists have also formulated certain models of communication on the basis of integrating certain elements of communication. In particular, E.A. Schegloff lists seven such aspects which are coated by Asha Kaul (2002). They include:

- A turn-taking system which allocates turns to the speakers and states that: (i) the current speaker selects the one to talk next (by asking questions/tag questions, etc.) or (ii) the speaker who self-selects continues speaking for a whole turn.
- Adjacency pairs, which are categories comprising two closely related pairs in which given one, the other follows, for example, question-answer, complement-acceptance, greeting-greeting, etc.
- Intermediate sized structures (stories, jokes, etc.).
- Topics which are content oriented and make sufficient contributions to the conversation.
- A structural organization which studies conversation as a linear progression consisting of a beginning, a middle and a closing section, is interspersed with certain devices which mark the shift from one section to another.
- Turn construction mechanism.
- Super ordinate system.

The ethno-methodologists have dealt with certain spoken and unspoken rules of communication about topical shift which sensitize the participants. The scholars have also used certain strategies to make the receivers gain focus or to ease the task of processing the message. H.P. Grice also provided certain cooperative principles of communication which deal with the range of referents and the context of communication. He observed that a conversational exchange is a succession of interrelated remarks which are the result of cooperative behaviour of the participants (sender and receiver). He also identified four maxims such as quantity, quality, relevance and manner which make the process of communication convenient to both the parties. A proper understanding of the models of communication is imperative in order to establish mutually beneficial relations and transactions through communication in modern society.

Impact of Communication

Melvin DeFleur (1970) highlights the impact of media on society which reads: "The communication process is utterly fundamental to all of our psychological and social processes. Without repetitively in acts of communication with our fellows, none of us could possibly develop the human mental processes and human social nature that distinguishes us from other forms of life."

In the age of media convergence, the media professionals discharge their duties in the virtual environment which is part of the present global communication. All communication media are interrelated sociologically, technologically and professionally. The contemporary generation of media professionals in print media, electronic media, new media, advertising, corporate communication, book publishing and other sectors are working with the help of electronic devices. Electronic processing and dissemination of data have become the essential features of media convergence.

Vilanilam (2005) explains the interrelationship among the media in the age of media convergence thus: "Film and video editing is done electronically. Advertising agencies and PR firms make use of electronic processing of data; and book publishers use electronic processing, editing and printing, including Desktop Publishing (DTP) systems. Every medium is related to every other medium. Electronics is part of the print media as reports are processed on computers and transferred electronically to a main information bank from where they can be recalled and edited, processed again, photo-composed and made part of the page to be electronically prepared for offset printing. The phenomenon of compunication (computerized communication) is part of every medium's operation on the practical plane. Most pieces of equipment in the modern media world are electronically operated. The 'global village' which Marshall MacLuhan spoke of in the 1960s has become a reality, at least in the technical sense, in the richer parts of the world. In a sociological sense too, there is interdependence in the media."

In the new age of information revolution, the ownership of mass media pattern is subjected to several changes. At present, chain ownership (means the same media company owns numerous outlets in a single medium), cross media ownership (means the same company own several media outlets), conglomerate ownership (means the ownership of several businesses, one of which is a media business) and vertical integration (means a media company monopolizes the production of the ingredients that go into the making of media products) are prominently found all over the world. In the present age of cross media, conglomerate and vertical integration ownership continues while media monopolization ultimately leads to the phenomenon of suppression of media freedom. Conglomeration and corporate mergers are witnessed in the present times especially in the US. Scholars have noted that mere diversification of ownership will not ensure diversity of news, views, programmes and services.

In the age of commercialization of media, competitive communication has become the order of the day. The media institutions to ignore the cause of truth and public interest and distort the truth for commercial advantages. The present trend of media ownership concentration in fewer hands is not conducive to the principles of welfare state, good governance, positive media management and protection of public interest. The communication system in India is not conducive for meaningful social communication since it caters to the needs of the creamy layer of the total population. The mass media in India and elsewhere have also become 'class media' and promote the social myth of caste superiority through various outputs. The media professionals also represent the privileged sections of society since they are required to perform the duty of 'media executives' and 'sellers of products'.

Media critic Noam Chomsky (1989) comments: "The media serve the interest of state and corporate power, which are clearly linked. The mainstream media not only allow the agenda of news to be bent in accordance with state's demands and criteria of utility; they also accept the presuppositions of the state without question."

The observation made by Chomsky and other media critics is also true of most Indian and Foreign media which are owned by the economic powers which rule the state. Media contents are primarily governed by the market forces, political pressures, business interests, casteist forces, government censorship, media regulations and other considerations which have deprived the people their right to free, fair and fearless communication. Development communication has become the biggest casualty in the age of media imperialism.

Vilanilam (2005) comments on the media output thus: "The sociological view of all media output is that all of it, despite claims of truthfulness and a realistic reflection of society, is more a construction than an exact reflection of reality. And this constructed reality has the stamp of the intellect, technology, economics, politics, culture and history of the environment where it is constructed. Despite their claim to the contrary, journalists and other communicators in society are not entirely 'free agents' as they cannot be totally free from their professional and social environment."

Summary

The growth of communication has undergone several stages including the age of stone writing to social media in the world. The objectives of communication are many and varied, depending upon the groups of people addressed and the context in which it is practiced. The spectrum of communication is very vast and defies any single definition. Communication is indeed a fundamental individual and collective necessity. It is practiced all over the globe at all times in order to facilitate proper understanding between the source of communication and beneficiaries of communication. Communication is an important exercise which facilitates mobilization of ideas, experiences and resources in the modern society. Communication facilitates expansion of knowledge, enrichment of experience and development of skills which are required for the sustainable development of the mankind. Communication is also a multi-faceted activity which has brought about intellectual revolution in the world. Communication has brought the people and organizations together and facilitated mutual understanding, interaction, transaction and progress across the world. All spheres of human life need active communication support for better development of the individuals, institutions and communities. Communication is a never ending mission which serves the whole world in several ways.

2

Basics of Communication Policy

Introduction

In modern society, policy formulation assumes great significance since it provides sound ideological and operational norms and guidelines to the elected representatives, administrators, professionals and other stakeholders of management and development in all spheres of human life. A policy is the blueprint which enables the various administrators and implementers to do the right things in the right time by following the right methods in order to serve the mankind. There are general policies and specific policies which facilitate proper understanding of the basic ideological and operational aspects concerning governance. Policies are made by the elected representatives, governing council, board of management and other bodies in modern society. Communication policies are also made all over the world to put the media organizations in the right track and enable the media professionals to follow the best methods while discharging their day-to-day duties. Hence, general policies and communication policies are essential in modern society. In this section, types of public policy, factors determining policy formulation, stakeholders of policy formulation, need for communication policy, communication policy at the global level, communication policy at the national level and evaluation of the communication policy are primarily discussed.

Types of Public Policy

Every profession demands a well-defined policy framework in order to educate, organize and direct the professionals properly. A policy is also required to facilitate the development of right vision and professional perspective among the professionals who are required to build and sustain the profession on the basis of sound ideological foundation. A policy is also a mechanism which is employed to realize the goals of a profession. A policy is also a blue print which indicates the desired course of action to achieve particular objects or goals. Policies are made by the seasoned, specialized and competent persons who are directly associated with the top management in every governmental or private organization.

Anderson (1976) defines a policy as 'a goal directed or purposive course of action followed by an actor or a set of actors in an attempt to deal with a public problem.'

Dunn (1981) states: 'A policy is a long series of more or less related choices, including decisions not to act, made by government bodies and officials.'

A policy is required in every government set up or corporate house in order to facilitate the delivery of goods and services in accordance with well defined operational framework. It is, therefore, a formally articulated goal that the government intends pursuing with society or with a societal group.

A policy can be defined as a proposed course of action of individual, a group, an institution or government to realize a specific objective or purpose within a given environment. The policy lays down a well-defined and approved framework within which the organizational goals are set to be accomplished. The goals and obligations of an organization are concretized in the policy goals which set the administrative wheels in motion. The policy formulation is the foremost management function of every organization. According to Berle, A. and Means, G. (1932), 'the essence of public administration is policy-making'. Diock and Dimock (1936) define it as 'the consciously acknowledged rules of conduct that guide administrative decisions'.

Generally, the policies are categorized into regulatory, distributive and re-distributive, according to Theodre Lowi (1964). The regulatory policies are binding on the part of administrators and general publics. The distributive policies facilitate the supply of goods and services to the general publics. Re-distributive policies normally take care of re-arranging one or more of the basic schedules of social and economic rewards. The government collects revenue from various stakeholders and distributes the goods and services which benefit the society.

Donna Kerr (1976) has referred to rule policies and goal policies. The rule policies stipulate that public and private organizations are required to adhere to certain norms and guidelines framed by the various agencies which intend to safeguard public interest. The goal policies are aimed at achieving certain goals and reaching certain targets in the interest of society. The public policies provide the meaningful basis for the conduction of administrative, welfare and developmental activities in modern society. The ways and means of achieving the goal varies from system to system. A policy ultimately enables the administrators to adopt an appropriate courses action which benefits the people. Policy formulation is necessary prior to every action in all modern organizations. The processes of management and development can be perfected on the basis of meaningful policy formulation in modern organizations. Hence, a public policy lays down the framework within which the organizational goals are set to be accomplished. The goals, functions and responsibilities of modern organizations are concretized in the policy goals which set the wheels of management and development in motion.

Frohock (1979) identifies two more sets of policies, namely—capitalization and ethical. The capitalization policies refer to the federal government providing funds to business and government both local and state in order to increase the productive capacity of various public institutions. The ethical policies are intended to regulating public actions which involve moral or ethical issues. The purpose of such policies is to increase the productive capacity of various public institutions which serve the mankind in different spheres of human life. The goods and services are delivered to the people under such policies. In particular, the ethical policies are based on certain healthy norms and guidelines which demonstrate the social concern of the service providers.

There are certain implications of public policy which refers to the action or decisional pattern by public administrators on a particular issue over a period of time. The public policy basically involves some form of government action regarding any issue or problem. It has a legal sanction behind it. It is potentially mandatory in nature and is binding on all public servants and citizens. Basically, public policies are different from the policies formulated by the private organizations. In case of private organizations, the governing council or board of management is the most competent authority to make the policies which are implemented by the community of employees.

The official policy-makers are legally empowered to formulate the policies in public and private sectors. The legislators are the foremost law makers in a political system. In reality, the legislature consents to laws that are originated by political parties ensure groups, framed by bureaucrats and introduced in the legislature by the government. In a Communist government, the legislature merely ratifies the decisions made by the high command or politburo within the Communist party. In a parliamentary democracy, a mass of legislation is made under the powers delegated to the elected representatives.

The executive is responsible for the implementation of the policy decisions. The judiciary reviews the appropriateness of policies in times of conflict of interest. Basically, the judicial review is the power of courts to determine the constitutionality of the decisions and actions of the legislature and executive and to declare them null and void if such decisions and actions are not in tune with the constitutional provisions. The pressure groups also play a major role in the policy-making process in democratic societies.

The public and private institutions normally formulate policies in order to achieve the goal of good governance. The public policies are made by the legislative bodies while the private policies are made by the governing councils. The public policies are made by the competent authorities in a political system, namely elected representatives, administrators, judges and other authorities. The public policy also refers to the action or decisional pattern adopted by the public administrators on a particular issue over a period of time. The public policy has the advantage of legislative approval even though it is either positive or negative in form. A policy involves a decision by the government officials on the basis of constitutional provisions. The private organizations also make policies which are in accordance with the well established work culture.

Factors Determining Policy Formulation

There are several factors which determine the policy-making under normal circumstances. Prominent among them include—culture of the land, history of the nation, political system, economic system and so on. The political, executive, administrative and technical dimensions of policy-making are constantly examined by the scholars. The policy formulation in practice often overlapses with the policy decision stage. A policy decision involves action by the officials concerned and approval of the legislative body or governing council. A policy is liable for approval or disapproval. It takes such forms as the enactment of legislation or issuance of an executive order if it is found positive by the competent authorities. The decision-makers also reject a policy if it is not in accordance with the constitutional norms and well established guidelines of management.

The prevailing political culture has a definite bearing on the policy-making process. A political culture oriented more to the pasts than to the future may sanctify age old traditions, customs and social moves in a pluralistic society like India than in the United States, a country whose culture is more future-oriented, adaptable and innovative. In the participant political culture, citizens sensitize the policy-makers and prevail upon them to formulate people-friendly policies. Government and public policy is viewed as controllable by the citizens especially in a participant political culture. In a democratic society, people have a right to prevail upon the government to improve their living standards by formulating progressive public policies.

The participation of the people in the policy formulation process is encouraged in a democracy. In a parochial political culture, citizens have little awareness, orientation and opportunity with respect to policy formulation. In a developing country like India, the people are not properly oriented towards the political system and mechanisms of policy-making. In America, the citizens have a high level political awareness, information and orientation with respect to their right to participation in the policy-making process. The participation of the people in the policy formulation in a parochial political culture is almost non-existent and government is of little concern to most of the people. In the participant political culture, the citizens are enabled to exercise their rights and influence government action as a matter of participatory democracy.

The prevailing socio-economic conditions also affect the policy formulation process invariably. The social and economic conditions of the people are related to the political activities including people's participation in the policy formulation process. The way in which socio-economic conditions influence the policy-making process are subjected to considerable analysis. The social status and economic development of the people shape the political culture, process and policy outcomes. The levels of literacy, awareness, social change, economic progress, political modernization, urbanization, industrialization, media exposure and empowerment matter most in shaping policy outcomes in modern society.

The public policy is known for certain characteristics, namely—legal authority, universality and imposition of punishment to the violators of policy. Scholars have examined the relationship between public policy and governmental institutions across the globe. There is a definite relationship between the government structure and policy outcomes. The multitude of problems, barriers to collection of information, personal characteristics of decision-makers, structural difficulties and deviant behaviour of individual administrators usually block the rational decision-making. The policy-makers are required to take into account the alternatives and values while making policies. The rational model of policy-making expects the policy-makers to take every issue into considerations and make meaningful decisions which facilitate sound delivery of goods and services.

Lindblom identifies the two advantages of 'incrementalism' in the process of policy formulation. First, if the decision-maker proceeds through a succession of small incremental changes, he has the advantage of avoiding serious alterations. Second, this method is truly reflective of the policy-making process in democratic states which operate chiefly by means of consensus and gradualism. Amitai Etzioni (1993) has argued that incremental changes are not sufficient and innovation is absolutely essential. Hence, Etzioni suggests a mixed scanning approach, combining elements of the rational method with the incrementalism which would focus on those areas in which certain formations are ignored.

Stakeholders of Policy Formulation

There are several stakeholders of policy formulation in modern society. The official policy-makers are those who are elected by the people directly to the Panchayat Raj Institutions (PRIs), state legislatures and national parliament in a country like India. The official policy makers are legally empowered to make policies which are mandatory from implementation point of view. The elected representatives perform the task of making policies, laws, rules and regulations in a political system at various levels and at different stages. They enjoy the benefit of independent decision making powers. The ruling party is required to make policies pertaining to public administration, national development, national security and so on. The ruling party has the opportunity to get any measure of its choice passed by the legislatures. The policy proposals are ratified in the legislature on the basis of systematic deliberations and active participation of legislatures. In a parliamentary system, a mass of legislation is made under the powers delegated to the ministers and elected representatives.

The executive is responsible for providing administrative support for the policy formulation. In parliamentary countries, all public policies should be approved by the cabinet and implemented by the executive bodies at various levels. In the developing countries, the executive probably has even more influence in the process of public policy-making. The executive plays a major role in policy formulation in the absence of strong bureaucratic base under the normal circumstances. In such countries, the pressure groups have limited opportunities for participation due to their lack of privilege, sophistication and coordination. The executive is also expected to act in conformity with the constitution, statutes, judicial decisions and other factors.

The administrative agencies also play a major role in the process of public policy-making even though they vary with respect to hierarchy, autonomy, size and so on. As a matter of fact, the administrators are required to execute the policies and implement the programmes which are approved by the legislature and executive bodies. The administrators who represent the creamy layor are also associated with the public policy formulation in several ways. The elected representatives and executives are not permanently associated with various government departments. But the administrators remain in the government departments for quite a long time and exercise great influence in the public policy-making process. In reality, the initiative for policy legislation originates from the administrators under the normal circumstances since the administrators are constantly in touch with the people. They are also aware of the feasibility of the policies at the stage of implementation on the basis of practical exposure and first hand experience. Sometimes, the administrators contribute immensely for the policy-making process on the basis of their practical exposure and administrative competence. In a country like India, the civil servants have a major say in the policy-making process since they play an advisory role. They collect authentic data, advise the elected representatives and select policy alternatives which enrich the process of public policy-making.

The judiciary does not have the power, privilege and competence to make any law or formulate any public policy. But the judicial organizations have the power of judicial review on the basis of well established constitutional provisions and previously decided cases. The judicial organizations have the capacity to thoroughly examine the relevance, adequacy and appropriateness of the public policies with due respect to constitutional obligations and public interest. They can also affect the nature, content and extent of public policy through exercise of the powers of judicial review and statutory interpretation in cases brought before them by the aggrieved parties. Certain public policies are also contested in the court of law through public interest litigations. In times of political omissions and commissions, the courts are approached to interpret and decide the relevance of legislative provisions and contents of public policies. The judiciary has played a crucial role in the formulation of public policies in India and other countries. In India, the judicial activism is constantly increasing over a period of time. The judicial organizations are called upon to facilitate the formulation of meaningful, positive and constructive public policies which benefit the people.

The pressure groups also play a major role in sensitizing the policy makers, administrators, professionals and the general publics on the pros and cons of public policies formulated from time to time at various levels by the competent authorities. The pressure groups enjoy a place of pride in a democratic system as watch dogs of public interest. There are more active pressure groups in the developed countries when compared to the pressure groups in developing and under developed countries. The pressure groups also enjoy the social and constitutional support in sensitizing the various stakeholders of public policy formulation in modern society. They can also utilize the media to formulate public opinion concerning the formulation of public policies. The pressure groups can also approach the judiciary for necessary intervention in times of need. The pressure groups are also free to organize the masses and conduct peaceful agitations for want of constructive public policies in times of need. Hence, the pressure groups are free to intervene indirectly in the process of public policy formulation as a matter of social responsibility in a democratic set up.

The political parties also play a vital role in the formulation of public policies in modern society. They are free to perform the function of 'interest aggregation' in a democratic set up. The political parties can also discuss at length various public policies and throw light on the strengths and weaknesses of public policies outside the legislature as a matter of social responsibility. The way in which the political parties 'aggregate' interest is affected by the number of parties. In case of bi-party systems such as the United States and Great Britain, the political parties are free to organize debates, discussions, agitations and other democratically tested and tried methods of public opinion formation and sensitization of stakeholders responsible for public policy formulation. In case of multiparty systems, the political parties naturally do less aggregating and act as the representatives of fairly narrow sets of interest. In India, the regional political parties are always wedded to the cause of regional development while the national political parties deliberate upon issues concerning the welfare and progress of the country. Generally speaking, the political parties have a broad range of policy concerns than the interest groups or pressure groups. Naturally, the ruling parties formulate public policies in accordance with the election manifestos or party ideological convictions.

In a democracy, the media institutions constitute the fourth estate besides legislature, executive and judiciary. The media institutions have a social responsibility of functioning as the voice of the people in a democracy. The media can also present their opinions on various aspects of public policy formulation as a matter of social concern. The media can also place facts, figures, ideas and guidelines with respect to several issues concerning the public policy formulation from time to time. The media professionals can also air their views and sensitize the various players in order to facilitate wide discussion and public opinion formation with respect to public policy formulation. In India, the media institutions played a crucial role in facilitating meaningful public policy formulation in times of need.

The individual citizens are also free to exercise their right to information, participation, agitation and progress in a democratic system. The individual citizens can also make use of several opportunities and contribute their opinions pertaining to public policy formulation on vital issues concerning governance, management and development of the nation. The individual citizens can make use of the media and air their views. They can also form associations to fight against wrong policies, programmes and actions as per the constitutional provisions. The citizens are also free to approach the judiciary through public interest litigations and prevail upon the judicial authorities to intervene and set things right in the interest of natural justice. The citizens are also free to make use of the elections and prevail upon the political parties to formulate appropriate public policies after the elections.

Charles Lindblom observes: "The most conspicuous difference between authoritarianism and democratic regimes is that democracies choose their top policy makers in genuine elections." The elections provide necessary opportunities to the people to exert influence on public policy formulation. The people are free to contact the political leaders and officials who matter most from the point of view of public policy formulation. In a democracy, the political parties including the ruling parties cannot go against the wishes of the people who are the masters with respect to public policy formulation.

Public policy formulation is indeed a cooperative endeavour and a collective effort in modern governments and organizations. There are many stakeholders who contribute their mite for the public policy formulation. The competent authorities are free to collect ideas, consolidate ideas and correlate the ideas in order to formulate a comprehensive public policy which benefits the society. The public policies become acceptable, feasible and implementable if they are based on authentic data, public aspirations, constitutional provisions and ground realities. The institutional and individual factors always matter most from the point of view of public policy formulation which is a collective effort in which several stakeholders participate actively. In India, the Parliament is the supreme public policy-making body concerning the national governance, security, management, development and so on. The state legislatures are also competent bodies to make public policies concerning provincial administration and regional development. The Panchayati Raj Institutions (PRIs) are at liberty to make policies concerning development administration and grassroots development in the rural and tribal areas.

Apart from government institutions, the educational institutions, social organizations, literary organizations, cultural organizations, trade unions, non-government organizations and other agencies also exercise much influence over the public policy-making process of India at different levels. The individuals basically constitute the democracy in letter and spirit. Hence, they are also enabled to play an active role in the process of public policy formulation. All these stakeholders are free to use truthful, non-violent and democratic means and facilitate public policy formulations in India.

Need for Communication Policy

Communication policies are sets of principles and norms established to guide the behaviour of communication systems. Communication policies are formulated over a period of time in the context of social, political, economic, cultural and media environments. Communication policies exist in every society regardless of the pattern of governance. General and specific communication policies are formulated at many levels. According to UNESCO (1977) communication policies may be incorporated in the constitution or legislation of country; in overall national policies, in the guidelines for individual administrations, in professional codes of ethics as well as in the constitutions and operational rules of particular communication institutions.

Matsuda *et al.* (1993) have observed that different media philosophies would, of course, respond differently to this question. Authoritarian media policies often follow the dictates of tradition. In multinational imperial systems such as the pre-modern Islamic and European empires, the level of tolerance for religious and ethnic differences was relatively high. The libertarian media policies tend to value free speech above politically correct speech. Proponents of a ban on hate speech, however, argue that it is equivalent to crying fire in a crowded theatre, thus constituting a 'clear and present danger.' The communitarian media policies face a different set of problems in ethnic and religious conflicts. By definition, such policies value one religion or language or ethnicity over others because they consider it of vital importance to their national unity. The totalitarian media policies, by contrast, leave little room for international or domestic remedies until the regime reaches its point of self-destruction. The introduction of market forces in China, Iran, the Philippines, the former Soviet Union, and Eastern Europe suggests, however, that a civil society may emerge sooner or later even under the tightest of controls. The national policies are often formulated in the context of global forces and policies.

In reality, there is no global sovereign government comparable to national governments from the point of view of formulating a global communication policy. But, there is a set of players or stakeholders on the global scene each taking part in formulating policies that inevitably enhance or constrain national governments in the pursuit of their goals. The key stakeholders of global communication policy-making include—states, markets, pressure groups, financial groups, civil societies, and media. States regulate, markets allocate, lobbies persuade, civil societies resist and mobilize, financial institutions accumulate, and the media de/legitimate policies. It is in the context of such forces and policies as well as their respective media outlets (state, public, commercial, community, advertising, pressure group, and trade and investment media) that global, national, and local discourses take place.

The communication policy of a country is formally presented in the form of an official document which is ratified in the national parliament. Some countries have not officially declared their communication policies but these policies are reflected in the expert committee reports, judgments of various courts, declarations of civil society or internal policy set by the various communications media. Cuilenberg and Mcquail (2003) identify three phases of communication policies paradigms that express the conceptual details in order to facilitate better understanding of public interest. These phases are identified from the mid-nineteenth century to the beginning of the Second World War duly characterized by piece meal accumulation of measure, with varying aims, means and scope. The second phase between Second World War and 1980s characterized public service media paradigms and shaped certain normative policies of communication media. The third phase began with the liberalization, privatization and globalization of media which took place in the 1990s. The communication policies were expressed in terms of economic and technological terms by several countries according to Chakravarthy and Sarikakis (2007).

Communication policies are formulated formally and informally across the globe depending upon the political ideology, environment, culture and established means and mechanisms. The communication policy decides the nature of media management and delivery of goods and services by the media institutions. The public media institutions are required to comply with the constitutional obligations, ethical norms and governmental policy considerations. The private media institutions are managed according to the whims and fancies of the market forces in the age of globalization. But the public and private media organizations are bound to follow the well defined communication policy of a particular nation or state in order to prevent the violation of ethical and professional norms. Hence communication policy formulation is undertaken by all the national governments in order to prevent the conflict of interest and safeguard public interest.

Communication Policy at the Global Level

A policy is usually described as a principle or rule to guide decisions and achieve rational outcome(s). The term is not normally used to denote what is actually done; this is normally referred to as either procedure or protocol. Policies are generally adopted by the highest decision-making body of an organization concerned. The governing council of an organization examines the procedures or protocols which would be developed and adopted by the management and other employees of an organization. A policy can be considered as a statement of intent or a commitment which makes the decision-makers accountable for the policy adopted by the organization. Communication policies are sets of principles and norms established to guide the behaviour of communication systems. The communication policy lays emphasis on the communication system, its components and the functions.

Communication policies which are formulated at the global level normally affect all countries or at least concern several countries of a region. The policy should also cater to the needs of international community. The policy-makers are required to identify the characteristics of the people involved in a communication system and especially the audiences it is aimed at. This area of concern may be taken for granted, for example, the entire nation is the audience, but frequently such a global approach will prove illusory and detrimental to meeting the many communication needs of different parts of the population. There may be a need to consider various minorities or even majorities, which under prevailing conditions do not have adequate access to communication, for example, rural populations, the lower working classes, and women. It is equally important to consider who is presently left outside existing communication policies. The non-audiences or excluded audiences may be as significant for policies as the presumed audiences themselves.

The international communication policy cuts across established administrations across the globe and demands meaningful co-ordination which is required for their concretization and translation into planning. It also calls for endorsement by the highest authorities of the State. Because many media are economical only when applied on a large scale and integrated into the total process of social communication, coordination needs to be reflected throughout the political and administrative hierarchy. This is rarely possible unless authorized from the top. At the same time, it is important that the concepts of communication policy and communication planning should not be equated with constraint and censorship, with dirigisme at the top. On the contrary, both should be concerned with assuring individual freedom of expression and communication within systems which are compatible with the needs for social dialogue.

The legislative bodies play an important role both through the laws concerning communication matters they may adopt and through the allocation of budgetary resources. Unless there is understanding of the significance of communication among legislators and close cooperation with others, there is little prospect for achieving the desired coordination and assuring the constructive role of communication in society. The international communication policy needs to be integrated into the social and economic objectives of the country and allocation of important resources required for a rational development of communication infrastructures call for decisions by the planning authorities.

The international federations of national associations, as well as of individuals, of professional and technical workers in the mass media intended to assist the members and to promote cooperation between them play an important role in the adoption of communication policy at the local level. The citizen has a direct stake in communication policies. The values and choices which guide communication affect his personal interest. He is a communicator in his own right and requires access to the media for participation and expression.

The role of the economist is crucial though confined. His effort entails continuous attempts to encourage decision-makers to adopt organized approaches to decision-making and to return to basic data for each decision. The economist is required to develop appropriate techniques for collecting data and analyzing the results in terms which can readily based on those who make policy decisions. The Mac Bride Commission (1982) submitted a report which called for the development of communication system at the global level in order to promote necessary dialogue for the development as a central component of both communication and development policies. The Commission stated that the implementation of national policies should be carried out through three complementary communication patterns:

- First, from decision-makers towards different social sectors to transmit information about what they regard as necessary changes in development actions, alternative strategies and the varying consequences of the different alternatives.
- Second, among and between diverse social sectors in a horizontal information network to express exchange views on their different demands, aspirations, objective needs and subjective motivations.
- Third, between decision-makers and all social groups through permanent participatory mechanisms for two-way information flows to elaborate development goals and priorities and make decisions on utilization of resources.

The Commission also recommended that special attention should be given to the use of non-technical language and comprehensible symbols, images and forms to ensure popular understanding of development issues and goals. Development information supplied to the media should be adapted to prevailing news values and practices, which in turn should be encouraged to be more receptive to development needs and problems. The Commission suggested that the national governments should devise policy instruments at the national level in order to evaluate the positive and negative social implications of the introduction of powerful new communication technologies. The specialists favoured that setting up national mechanisms would promote participation and discussion of social priorities in extension of new communication technologies.

Communication and cultural policies should ensure that creative artists and various grassroots groups can make their voices heard through the media. The innovative uses of film, television or radio by people of different cultures should be studied such experiments constitute a basis for continuing cultural dialogue, which could be furthered by agreements between countries and through international support. The Commission provided certain guidelines with respect to advertising content and the values and attitudes it foster in accordance with national standards and practices. Such guidelines should be consistent with national development policies and efforts to preserve cultural identity. Particular attention should be given to the impact of media on children and adolescents. In this connection, various mechanisms such as complaint boards or consumer review committees might be established to afford the public the possibility of reacting against advertising which they feel inappropriate.

While acknowledging the need of the media for revenues, ways and means should be considered to reduce the negative effects that the influence of market and commercial considerations have in the organization and content of national and international communication flows. The consideration is given to changing existing funding patterns of commercial mass media. In this connection, reviews could be made of the way in which the relative role of advertising volume and costs pricing policies, voluntary contributions, subsidies, taxes, financial incentives and supports could be modified to enhance the social function of mass media and improve their service to the community.

The Commission also called upon the developing countries to pay particular attention to:

- The correlation between education, scientific and communication policies, because their practical application frequently overlaps.
- The creation in each country of one or several centres for the collection and utilization of technical information and data, both from with the country and from abroad.
- To secure the basic equipment necessary for essential data processing activities.
- The development of skills and facilities for computer processing and analysis of data obtained from remote sensing.

The developed countries were called upon to foster exchanges of technical information on the principle that all countries have equal rights to full access to available information. It is increasingly necessary, in order to reduce inequalities in this field, to promote cooperative arrangements for collection, retrieval, processing and diffusion of technological information through various networks, regardless of geographical or institutional frontiers. The communication values as truthfulness, accuracy and respect for human rights are not universally applied at present. Higher professional standards and responsibility cannot be imposed by decree, nor do they depend solely on the goodwill of individual journalists, who are employed by institutions which can improve or handicap their professional performance. The self-respect of media professionals, their integrity and inner drive to turn out work of high quality are of paramount importance. It is this level of professional dedication, making for responsibility, which should be fostered by news media and journalists' organizations. In this framework, a distinction may have to be drawn between media institutions, owners and managers on the one hand, and journalists on the other.

All professions including mass communication have developed their own codes of professional ethics which are adopted voluntarily in many countries by professional groups. The adoption of codes of ethics at national and in some cases, at the regional level is desirable, provided that such codes are prepared and adopted by the profession itself without governmental interference. Conventional standards of news selection and reporting, and many accepted news values, need to be reassessed if readers and listeners around the world are to receive a more faithful and comprehensive account of events, movements and trends in both developing and developed countries.

The media professionals who are working in different parts of the world are required to undergo language training and gain necessary acquaintance with the history, institutions, politics, economics and cultural environment of the country or region in which they will be serving. The press and broadcasters in the industrialized world should allot more space and time to reporting events about foreign countries and news from the developing world. Also, the media in developed countries especially the gatekeepers, editors and producers of print and broadcasting media who select the news items to be published or broadcast should become more familiar with the cultures and conditions in developing countries. The professionals are called upon to develop sound vision and equip themselves with necessary skills and competence in order to do absolute justice to their role. The professional independence and integrity of all those involved in the collection and dissemination of news, information and views to the public should be safeguarded.

The UNESCO convened a series of round tables at which journalists, media executives, researchers and jurists could periodically review problems related to the protection of journalists and proposed additional appropriate measures to this end. The media were required to contribute towards promoting the just cause of peoples struggling for freedom and independence and their right to live in peace and equality without foreign interference. Communication needs in a democratic society should be met by the extension of specific rights such as the right to be informed, the right to inform, the right to privacy, the right to participate in public communication all elements of a new concept, and the right to communicate. The report also highlighted that censorship or arbitrary control of information should be abolished. In areas where reasonable restrictions may be considered necessary, these should be provided for by law, subject to judicial review and in line with the principles enshrined in the United Nations Charter, the Universal Declaration of Human Rights and the International Covenants relating to human rights, and in other instruments adopted by the community of nations.

The Commission recommended that effective legal measures should be designed to limit the process of concentration and monopolization, circumscribe the action of transnational's by requiring them to comply with specific criteria and conditions defined by national legislation and development policies, reverse trends to reduce the number of decision-makers at a time when the media's public is growing larger and the impact of communication is increasing, reduce the influence of advertising upon editorial and policy and broadcast programming, seek and improve models which would ensure greater independence and autonomy of the media concerning their management and editorial policy regardless of public and private ownership of media. The international communication policy emphasized that women and weaker sections should be enabled to gain adequate access to communication means and those images of them and of their activities are not distorted by the media or in advertising.

Communication policy-makers at the global level should give far greater importance to devising ways whereby the management of the media could be democratized while respecting national customs and characteristics by associating the following categories: (a) journalists and professional communicators; (b) creative artists; (c) technicians; (d) media owners and managers; (e) representatives of the public. Such democratization of the media needs the full support and understanding of all those working in them and this process should lead to their having a more active role in editorial policy and management. The national news agencies were called upon to extend mutually beneficial services and facilitate the development of non-aligned news agencies pool in order to manage the general exchange on a regular basis of radio, TV programmes and films.

The international experts also stated that the national communication policies should be consistent with adopted international communication principles and should seek to create a climate of mutual understanding and peaceful co-existence among nations. Countries should also encourage their broadcast and other means of international communication to make the fullest contribution towards peace and international cooperation and to refrain from advocating national, racial or religious hatred and incitement to discrimination, hostility, violence or war. All forms of cooperation among the media, the professionals and their associations, which contribute to the better knowledge of other nations and cultures, should be encouraged and promoted. These recommendations were made by the Mac Bride Commission in 1982 for the betterment of media services across the globe.

Communication Policy at the National Level

The press in India played a historical role in the liberation of the country from European colonialism. The national leaders were aware of the power of communication and accorded high priority for mass communication in India. The importance of the role of communication for national development was fully understood by the national leaders before independence. The Indian National Congress led by Mahatma Gandhi set up a sub-committee on communication under the National Planning Committee to prepare grounds for the development of communication system for independent India. The framers of the Constitution of India accorded high priority to the freedom of speech and expression and incorporated several progressive provisions for the development of independent media system in India. The First Five Year Plan document highlighted the need and importance of free, fair and fearless media policy for national development. The founders of modern India realized the importance of communication support for national development and established the Ministry of Information and Broadcasting which has several media units across the country.

With the target of development communication, the new government adopted the recommendations of the erstwhile National Planning Committee as the mainstay of its communication policies. "The issue of using modern communication acquired high priority as a developmental resource during the Nehru era when the planners explored the prospects of using radio as a development agent, that is, for information and enlightening the people in the countryside and towns on developmental issue." The Government of India began radio broadcasting under the banner of 'Akashavani' which has emerged as the single largest broadcasting network in the world.

Several newspapers and periodicals also appeared in the post-independence era thanks to the progressive media policy of the government. The Directorate of Advertising and Visual Publicity co-ordinated the advertising services of the government and encouraged the print and electronic media. Many small and community based newspapers also received the patronage of the government and community. The government encouraged the media through publicity and advertising support for various national development endeavours. The state governments also established the department of information and publicity in order to bridge the communication gap between the government and people. The Indian Space Research Organization was developed by the government as a premier centre of satellite communication development in the country.

Pandit Jawaharlal Nehru was a great visionary and champion of media freedom. He firmly believed that India should have a democratized, decentralized and localized communication system in order to enlist the active participation of people in the process of nation building. In the post-independence era, the national leaders consciously adopted social responsibility theory of communication and contributed their mite for the expansion of communication system all over the country. In the post-Nehruvian era, visionary scientists like Vikram Sarabhai argued that India needs all possible technological know-how to educate the people about various developmental programmes.

Vikram Sarabhai and Kamla Chaudhury (1974) observed: "Our national goals involve leap-frogging from a state of economic backwardness and social disabilities attempting to achieve in a few decades a change which was incidentally taken centuries in other countries and in other lands. This involves innovation at all levels." Sarabhai argued on this premise that *television* be given special priority for accelerating national development. He believed that technology can help set a national agenda for 'implementing schemes of economic and social development……it is of particular significance for population living in isolated rural countries.'

Accepting that the western world used the new technology and innovation to spread consumer culture, Nehru called upon the scientists and the technologists to bend the same technology to achieve the Gandhian task of 'ending of poverty and ignorance and disease and inequality of opportunity.' Nehru showed an unambiguous indication of predilection towards the BBC style of autonomy. On a speech delivered on 'freedom of information' on March 5, 1962 Nehru said "The mass media which are very useful have an element of danger in them in that they may be distorted for private aim. The rich group (inside) or the rich nation (outside) can flood the country and the world through the mass media with its own view of things which may or may not be correct view." These words had turned out to be ominously true in the present world.

Indira Gandhi succeeded her father as the Prime Minister of India and strongly supported the ideas of Sarabhai which culminated in the launching of the momentous Satellite Instructional Television Experiment (SITE) in 1975-76 from the Space Application Centre located at Ahmedabad. It started beaming development oriented programmes to 2400 Indian villages. The software was designed according to the socio-cultural specificities of the areas concerned. It was a path breaking experiment in the field of development communication not only in India but also for the whole world. This experiment heralded a new era of development broadcasting in the Indian subcontinent. It was indeed a success story which demonstrated the vision of the national leaders regarding the role of media in the national development process. The Indian leaders did not formulate any specific communication policy but adopted progressive measures for the advancement of the country through active and creative communication support.

During the days of Indira Gandhi the infrastructure for television communication received a major boost. During 1984-85 over 120 television transmitters were installed in India. But as is a typical Indian trait, the SITE experiment in the Kheda district died a silent death with Sarabhai. "The Kheda Project itself was wound up under tremendous pressure of the new rural middle class which was carried away by the glitter and glamour of the new television software," according to Banerjee (2002).

The late Prime Minister of India Rajiv Gandhi also played a decisive role in the modernization of communication services in India. He was ably assisted by Sam Pitroda who revolutionized the management of telecommunication in India. Rajiv Gandhi realized the importance of autonomous media system in India and facilitated the scientific and technological advancement of electronic and new media system in India. Rajiv Gandhi was a great visionary who encouraged the fourth estate to play the role of watch-dog of public interest fearlessly. The attitude of Rajiv Gandhi towards communication was progressive and supportive.

P.V. Narasimha Rao and Manmohan Singh played a major role in the economic liberalization of India in 1990s. The duo brought about commendable reformation of Indian economy in general and media progress in particular. The Foreign Direct Investment (FDI) was encouraged by the national leaders which facilitated the remarkable growth of Indian media system. An era of private electronic media was witnessed during the last decade of 20th century. The successive Prime Ministers, namely P.V. Narasimha Rao, V.P. Singh, Chandrashekhar, I.K. Gujral, Devegowda, Vajapayee and Manmohan Singh attached great importance to media expansion in the country. The new media of communication flourished in the Indian soil and facilitated interactive communication in the country.

The Five Year Plans visualized the development and utilization of communication media in order to enlist active participation of people in the process of development through integrated media campaigns. The media laws, norms and guidelines underwent a drastic change under the leadership of various progressive Prime Ministers. The print media, electronic media and new media played a prominent role in the transformation of the national economy. The All India Radio and Doordarshan faced tough challenge from the private channels and improved their profile remarkably. The traditional and modern channels of communication were developed under the patronage of Government of India. New media were expanded all over the country and e-education, e-commerce, e-development, e-governance, e-medicine and other branches of development emerged in the new millennium. In the age of globalization, the communications media grew remarkably and gained lot of public recognition and criticism. The Indian government pursued the policy of progressive communication and encouraged the growth and development of both traditional and modern media.

Communication policy formulation is the prerogative of the government. Operationally, the government is responsible for analyzing the communication systems and operations which have a bearing on the well-being of the people. In India several communications media have emerged on the basis of technological revolution. Aravind Veermani (2000) writes: "A communication-information revolution requires a complete transformation of approach, from one which views telecommunication as a monopoly to be used for extracting rents for the government, to one which sees it as a revolutionary instrument for transforming India through empowerment of its citizens. A communication policy embodying such an approach can make India into an information technology power in the next two decades. The necessity for a regulatory system arises from the fact that parts of the communication system still resemble or approximate a natural monopoly. Rapid technological innovation is changing the situation from day-to-day. The Internet and Information Technology policies have followed each other in quick succession. The time may be ripe for a revolutionary new communication policy, which can make India an information technology power in the 21st century."

India has emerged as a media super power on account of the governmental patronage and community support. Since independence, there is no formulation of official communication policy in India. But, the Indian national leaders have adopted progressive unwritten communication policy which has led to the notable development of media system and operations in India. The Constitution of India has accorded a place of pride to the media freedom. Chanda Committee, Verghese Committee, Joshi Committee, Sen Gupta Committee, Paswan Committee, Pawar Committee and other Committees have consciously examined the need for Indian communication policy and guided the successive governments in the adoption of progressive media practices.

Evaluation of the Communication Policy

A systematic study of the policy-making process facilitates generation of adequate knowledge and understanding of the complexities of the interacting social, economic and political processes. The policy is a dependent variable since it is based on national culture, political system, economy and constitutional obligations. Scholars have examined the political and environmental factors which are associated with the policy-making process. They have pointed out that the study of public policy should be directed towards ensuring that government adopts appropriate policies to attain certain desirable social and economic goals.

Policy research has become an important aspect of contemporary scientific investigation since the appropriateness, relevance; significance and utility of the policy deserve systematic evaluation by the experts concerned. The policy makers and administrators are required to collect feedback from the people about the utility of the policies and bring about meaningful changes and modifications with due respect to public interest. The systems theory is found quite useful in understanding the policy-making process. However, this model is criticized for employing the value laden techniques of welfare economies which are based on the maximization of a clearly defined social welfare function.

Media experts have also identified the missing elements, namely—power, personnel and institutions in the process of policy-making. Scientific evaluation of the policy outcomes is undertaken with a view to assess the strengths and weaknesses of the policies concerned. In reality, the governmental decisions in all sectors of national development in general and media management in particular involve great social and developmental costs to the nation. In reality, all public policies including media policies affect the people of the country either directly or indirectly. The people have the right to know such decisions and actions if they are initiated by the government and media organizations as a matter of social accountability. In particular, the tax payers also have a right to know as to what extent the public money is correctly utilized by the government and media organizations in this age of transparency. These fundamental questions are now being raised by the policy analysts who are also required to build a body of scientific knowledge about the social concerns of the public policies.

A new branch of policy science has emerged in the world in order to take stock of the situation and suggest suitable changes and modifications to the public policies made by different competent authorities over a period of time. The development of policy science has created a body of policy analysts and enabled the various policy makers to understand the strengths, weaknesses, opportunities and threats of various public policies. Yehezkel Dror states: "Policy science can be partly described as the discipline that searches for policy knowledge which seeks general policy issue knowledge and policy-making knowledge and integrates them into a distinct study."

The emergence of a new branch of policy knowledge concerns itself with the entire spectrum of policy-making activities in all spheres of administration and development. It puts the search light on the ways and means of enrichment of public policies which would enable the policy makers and implementers achieve maximum success in modern organizations in their day-to-day administrative and developmental endeavours. The specialists have designed certain policy evaluation instruments with a view to ensure the adoption of the best policy by judicious evaluation of goals, values, aspirations, alternatives, costs and benefits on the maximum use of all available data, technologies and strategies. Scholars have formulated the extra rational aids to facilitate scientific and systematic policy analysis. A new body of policy science knowledge is developed by the scientific evaluation of public policies.

The evaluation of public policies is undertaken with a view to assess the contents and effects of public policies on those for whom they are intended. The policy evaluation is undertaken at formation stage, process stage and summative stage in modern governments and organizations. A new generation of policy analysts has emerged on the basis of systematic training and orientation in modern organizations. The policy impact is also assessed by the experts. Policy strategy evaluation is undertaken with a view to assess the relative effectiveness of programme strategies and variables. The policy project appraisal is undertaken on the basis of an assessment of individual projects through case study or case analysis method. The policy output and policy outcomes are systematically analyzed by the experts. The policy output refers to the quantifiable actions of the government which can be measured in concrete terms. But policy outcomes are also measured on the basis of the impact of public policies on the lives of the people. The scientific policy evaluation requires thorough knowledge of what was envisaged and what is accomplished on the part of the analysts. The cause and effect relationships are rigorously measured by the policy analysts on the basis of tested and tried parameters and approaches.

There are certain constraints of policy analysis which are encountered by the analysts. Uncertainty over policy goals, difficulty in determination of causality, complex policy inputs, diffused policy impacts, difficulties in data acquisition and other complexities of policy analysis are usually encountered by the experts. Practically, quantitative policy analysis is a challenging task that lies ahead of the analysts. But qualitative policy anaiysis is undertaken on the basis of scientific correlation of policy inputs and impacts by the analysts. The policy analysis is undertaken on the basis of questions, debates, observations, case analyses and other methods in the government organizations. The audit process involves the scientific evaluation of the budgetary appropriations that have been utilized economically by the government agencies or Non-Governmental Organizations (NGOs). The government departments prepare internal evaluation reports which are assessed by the external auditors. The commissions and committees are also constituted by the government organizations to assess the implications of public policies as and when required. The policy analysis has become inevitable in modern society in order to withdraw the obsolete policies and standardize the public policies on sound footing of knowledge, experience and expertise.

Summary

Policies are made in all public and private organizations with a view to facilitate meaningful delivery of goods and services on the basis of ethical considerations and service orientation. All modern professions demand sound policy framework in order to serve the mankind in the right direction. The policy makers formulate the policy and the executive is responsible for the implementation of the policy decisions. The judiciary reviews the appropriateness of policies in times of conflict of interest. There are various stakeholders of policy formulation in modern society. Communication policies are sets of principles and norms established to guide the behaviour of communication systems. Communication policies are formulated over a period of time in the context of social, political, economic, cultural and media environments. Communication policies which are formulated at the global level normally affect all countries or at least concern several countries of a region. The international communication policy cuts across established administrations across the globe and demands meaningful coordination which is required for their concretization and translation into planning. The Five Year Plans have emphasized active media intervention for integrated development of the country in India. The framers of the Constitution of India accorded high priority to the freedom of speech and expression and incorporated several progressive provisions for the development of independent media system in India. P.V. Narasimha Rao and Manmohan Singh played a major role in the economic liberalization of India in 1990s. Communication policy formulation is the prerogative of the government. Several committees have guided the successive governments in the adoption of progressive media policies. The imperativeness of a national communication policy is seldom questioned by anybody in the Indian Republic.

3

Globalization and World Media

Introduction

Globalization is driven by technological and economic changes, but it has cultural and political implications as well. The speed of transport and communication has increased throughout the 20th century. This kind of acceleration continues to exist in all sectors of the life in the age of globalization. The process of standardization has begun by nationalism and national economies and globalization entails comparability and shared standards where there were formerly none. Globalization has brought about interconnectedness wherein the media networks connecting people across continents are becoming denser, faster and wider every moment. The entire world is on the move, or so it might sometimes seem. Migration, business travel, international conferences and not least tourism have been growing steadily for decades, with various important implications for local communities, politics and economies. The process of globalization has affected the communications media institutions and operations decisively according to the findings of various studies concerning the relationship between globalization and world media. The salient features of globalization of economy, impact of globalization on media (print, electronic, film, NCTs, folk media), corporate advertising and corporate communication are examined in this section.

Globalization of Economy

Globalization is not a new phenomenon. The human civilization has witnessed three kinds of globalization till now. Buddha heralded the first phase of globalization in India 2500 years ago. He created the democratic culture for the first time in the world and brought about the empowerment of women and weaker sections in India by following truthful, non-violent and democratic means. He brought about the humanization of culture, polity, economy and so on for the first time and became the foremost maker of the universe on the basis of the principles of equality, liberty, fraternity and justice. The European colonial forces led by the British initiated the second phase of globalizaiion in the world. They conquered most of the countries in Asia, Africa, Latin America and elsewhere by using their manipulative tactics. They commercialized the culture, polity and economy across the world.

Karl Marx and Friedrich Engels (1848) in their Manifesto of the Communist Party noted: "Modern industry has established the world market. This market has given an immense development to commerce, to navigation, to communication by land. This development has in its turn, reacted on the extension of industry. The bourgeoisie resolved personal worth into exchange value, and in place of the numberless indefeasible chartered freedoms, has set up that single, unconscionable freedom—Free Trade." The bourgeoisie has through its exploitation of the world market given a cosmopolititan character to production and consumption in every country. To the great chagrin of Reactionists, it has drawn from under the feet of industry the national ground on which it stood. All old-established national industries have been destroyed or are daily being destroyed. They are dislodged by new industries, whose introduction becomes a life and death question for all civilized nations, by industries that no longer work up indigenous raw material, but raw material drawn from the remotest zones; industries whose products are consumed in every quarter of the globe. In place of the old local and national seclusion and self-sufficiency, we have intercourse in every direction, universal inter-dependence of nations."

The world 'globalization' is widely discussed in the present times by many scholars across the globe. The process of globalization has affected all spheres of human life in letter and spirit. There has been a growing body of research on the topic of globalization. Globalization is the increasing unification of the world's economic order through reduction of such barriers to international trade as tariffs, export fees and import quotas. The goal is to increase material wealth, goods and services through an international division of labour by efficiencies catalyzed by international relations, specialization and competition. In the age of globalization, the regional economies, societies, and cultures are integrated through communication, transportation, trade and other means. Globalization is the integration of national economies into the international economy through trade, foreign direct investment, capital flows, migration, the spread of technology and military presence. However, globalization is usually recognized as being driven by a combination of economic, technological, socio-cultural, political, and biological factors. The term can also refer to the transnational circulation of ideas, languages, or popular culture through acculturation. An aspect of the world which has gone through the process can be said to be globalized.

According to the Oxford English Dictionary, the word 'globalization' was first employed in a publication entitled 'Towards New Education in 1930', to denote a holistic view of human experience in education. An early description of globalization was penned by the founder of the Bible Student movement Charles Taze Russell who coined the term 'corporate giants' in 1897. The term began to be widely used by economists and other social scientists in 1960s. The term has been widely discussed by the community of economists since 1980s. The concept of globalization has inspired numerous competing definitions and interpretations, with antecedents dating back to the great movements of trade and empire across Asia and the Indian Ocean from the 15th century onwards according to the economic historians.

Traditional definitions of globalization focus on economics and the effects of multinational corporations. Cavanaugh and Mader (2002) referred to a number of factors that are identified with the term globalization. These factors include—hyper-growth and exploitation of the environment, privatization of public services, global cultural homogenization, promotion of consumerism, integration of national economies, corporate deregulation, and displacement of traditional nation-states by global corporate bureaucracies. Globalization is being driven by increasingly strong international market factors fuelled by organizations such as the World Trade Organization (WTO), International Monetary Fund (IMF) and UNESCO.

The United Nation's ESCWA (1996) states: "Globalization is a widely used term that can be defined in a number of different ways. When used in an economic context, it refers to the reduction and removal of barriers between national borders in order to facilitate the flow of goods, capital, and services and labour although considerable barriers remain to the flow of labour. Globalization is not a new phenomenon. It began towards the end of the nineteenth century, but it slowed down during the period from the start of the World War I until the third quarter of the twentieth century. This slowdown can be attributed to the inward-looking policies pursued by a number of countries in order to protect their respective industries, however, the pace of globalization picked up rapidly during the fourth quarter of the twentieth century."

Much of the current climate of international investment and global business is a direct result of global reconstruction, which followed World War II. Both the World Bank and the International Monetary Fund (IMF) were founded within a few years after the end of World War II. Critics of globalization say that capitalism is the driving force behind world economics. Globalization emerged as a buzzword in the 1990s, just as interdependence did in the 1970s. The end of the Cold War in 1989-91 brought about systematic institutionalization of globalization under the leadership of US. The Americans have led the third phase of globalization in the present times which has brought about the victimization of mankind.

The process of globalization becomes incomplete in the absence of technological development and application as a consequence of the marriage between post-industrialization and globalization, according to Castles (1998). Doreen Massey notes: "There is a power geometry of globalization in which 'some people are more in charge of than others; some initiate flows and movement, other's do not; some are more on the receiving-end of it than others; some are effectively imprisoned by it." Most scholars have acknowledged that in most situations, there is going to be an imbalance of power when dealing with two nations in the age of globalization.

According to Rantanen, the process of globalization has brought about homogenization and heterogenization. Homogenization refers to all those processes by which peoples of the world are incorporated into a single world society, global society, according to Albrow (1990).

Heterogenization, on the other hand, sees the effects of globalization as a complex set of interacting and often countervailing human, material, and symbolic flows that lead to diverse, heterogeneous cultural positioning and practices which persistently and variously modify established sectors of social, political, and cultural power, according to Lull (1995).

Schiller (1985) observes: "The impact of globalization on economy is widely studied by the scholars all over the world. This impact has reshaped the processes of world production, distribution, trade, development and financing. Expanding global transportation and telecommunications networks in recent decades have clearly enabled the Trans-National Corporations (TNCs) to decentralize their production and distribution networks while seeking higher profits in regions of the world with lower wages, rents, taxes, and government regulation. World trade and financing have also been profoundly affected by the transborder data flows that facilitate airline and hotel reservations, cash and capital transfers, and international trade in capital markets."

Globalization means not only the expansion of trade between countries, but the intensive division of labour is showing more and more production factors wandering, especially the mobile capital. Economic location competition is developing between countries. Globalization in the economic sector means a development which moves the world economy closer to the theoretical ideal of perfect markets, i.e. competition no longer takes place only within the framework of national states. The OECD perceives globalization as a process through which markets and production in various countries are becoming more and more interdependent, because of the dynamics of trade in goods and services and the movements of capital and technology. The new form of economic globalization, compared to the 19th century, is that not just trade, but enterprises themselves are crossing borders. National states have to entice the mobile capital, whereby the rule is that the better the image the higher the chances to attract foreign capital.

The driving force behind globalization is motivated by economic interests. According to Amnesty International (2000), "Of the 100 largest economies in the world, 51 are now global corporations; only 49 are countries. The developing nations have diminishing power to control mergers, take-overs and liquidations, may not know who plans to buy or sell a major industry or utility; a telephone, TV or water company may change ownership overnight. The developing nations are losing their national sovereignty and that human rights violations are taking place every moment across the world." Scholars have identified three dimensions of globalization—transnational economic activity, communication networks and increased tensions between (and within) cultural groups. The world has been fundamentally transformed after the late 1980s, but that the driving forces of both economic, political and cultural dynamics are transnational—and that this is now widely acknowledged.

Roland Robertson (1992) observes: "Globalization as a concept refers both to the compression of the world and the intensification of consciousness about the world as a whole. The compression of the world, in all of its forms, brings us closer to each other for better and for worse. The consciousness about these interconnections gives a sense of both opportunities and of vulnerability. This dual character of globalization—increased interconnectedness and increased awareness of it—can be studied from a myriad of empirical vantage-points. It would be perfectly feasible (and it is probably already being done somewhere) to write a dissertation on European reactions to the Asian bird-flu in 2006. The impact of globalization on tribal peoples in Malaysia has, moreover, long been a subject in anthropology. Human geographers write about the displacement of people in India as a result of globally driven economic deregulation. Many write about migration, again from a variety of perspectives. Others are concerned with the distribution of economic power in the global economy, or the distribution of symbolic or definitional power in the global media world; some write about standardization of goods and services as an outcome of the globalization of the economy, others about the spread of certain consumer preferences, yet others about the global tourist industry; while others again study international law, human rights as a consequence of globalization or the anti-globalization movement."

Friedman (1997) writes: "Globalization is really recent, and began only in the 1980s. As shown briefly already, this view betrays the beholder's poor knowledge of history. World-systems have existed earlier in the sense that people all over the world have participated, often involuntarily, in political and economic systems of a huge, often intercontinental scale. The European colonial era is the most obvious instance, but one might argue that the Roman Empire, encompassing as it did most of the known world (for Europeans), or the Aztec Empire, shared many of the characteristics of today's globalization."

Amartya Sen comments: "The production of wealth makes freedom actual and thereby is the essential prerequisite for the pursuit of all other human goods. Wealth should be a matter of global interest in order to prohibit a world where only a few wealthy nations have exclusively the conditions that make possible genuine freedom of choice. It is wealth that permits the development of freedom and freedom is the only condition under which a meaningful choice of other ends is possible. I agree with Aristotle that wealth is not a human end in itself. However, without wealth, at least wealthy societies, the possibility of choosing among a full range of other desirable ends is neither real nor actual. Although, the process of globalization may exert a levelling influence, such a levelling process would only limit meaningful choice of higher ends and thereby radically devalue the freedom which wealth permitted to develop. Again the question of whether the form of utilitarianism expressed in terms of global free markets has the power to mediate justly among the various conflicting claims of constituent interest groups, with different traditional value systems, within the global society must be examined. Cultural traditions may impose duties that have no status or a negative one in a global value system."

Grieco and Holmes (1999) comment: "Globalization has largely been driven by the interests and needs of the developed world. This is not unconnected with the fact that world developments have been increasingly characterized not by their growth dynamics but by their links to the process of globalization. Hence, the overwhelming character of globalization has made it compelling for some scholars to use various aspects of the global economy as units of analysis. Looking specifically at economic globalization, it can be measured in different ways. These centre on the four main economic flows that characterize globalization, namely—goods and services, workforce, migration rates and exports and imports."

Critics have argued that globalization is just a new word for economic imperialism or cultural Westernization. This view reduces the vast range of transnational processes to certain economic ones. Although it is tautologically true that rich countries are dominant, the situation is not static. China, India, South Korea and other formerly poor countries are emerging as equal players, and regional powers such as South Africa and Brazil. The direction of transnational flows is not unilateral: some things flow from north to south, others from south to north, and there is also considerable movement between east and west and within the south. Others have perceived that globalization means homogenization. This view is simplistic and usually misleading. Globalization is opposed to human rights since it has widened the gap between the rich and poor all over the world. Women and weaker sections have become the foremost victims of violation of human rights in the age of globalization.

Experience reveals that globalization is a threat to local identities since the market forces have controlled all spheres of human life and heralded a new era of commoditization in the world. Many countries in Asia, Africa, Latin America, Middle East and other continents have been adversely affected by the process of globalization which imposes certain restrictions on the local communities.

Gray (2003) comments: "We are witnessing a process of internationalization and regionalization rather than the emergence of one integrated world of rapid communication, transnational networks and global financial capital". Skeptics argue, further, that the nation-state remains the most important political entity, while others claim that state sovereignty is on the wane, and that multilateralism and transnational politics are replacing it. Skeptics also see a continuation of the classic North-South divide in terms of prosperity and power, while critics argue that inequalities are chiefly growing within and not between societies. The world has witnessed the continued or indeed increasing power of national identities and cultures, analysts describe hybrid ties and cosmopolitan orientations as an outcome of intensified interaction.

The people of different origins are enjoying the benefit of connectivity and the new age of communication revolution has led to probably more cultural mixing than ever before in human history. The farmers, workers, women and indigenous people have become highly vulnerable because of the adverse impact of globalization. The whole world is shrinking because of the increasing globalization and the geographical boundaries drawn between such domains are largely artificial and will be dispensed with when they are not needed. Scholars have identified the objective and subjective globalization over a period of time. The objective globalization means being incorporated into a global, or wide-ranging transnational system while the subjective globalization amounts to the acknowledgement of such processes taking place in the world. Globalization has also become a new way of life which has encouraged heterogeneity rather than uniformity or homogeneity. Scholars have assessed the impact of globalization and noted the positive and negative implications of globalization.

Klein (2002) has pointed out that the process of globalization concerns the relationship of globalization to neoliberal economics. Many countries that have complied with measures imposed by international agencies like the World Bank and the International Monetary Fund (IMF) have experienced a steep decline in *de facto* standards of living. Neoliberals is often associated with the global spread of human rights ideas rather than the global financial market. There is growing debate over the relationship between globalization and democracy. Many scholars, politicians and commentators are concerned about the loss of political power experienced by nation-states when so much economic power is diverted to the transnational arenas according to Roy (1999).

Amin (2004) has dealt with the relationship between poor and rich countries in the age of globalization and pointed out that the poor nations become poorer and the rich richer as a result of economic globalization. The major beneficiaries of globalization are the market forces which have controlled the global economy. The African countries are among the least globalized in terms of integration into the world economy. Their exports are modest, and foreign investment is considered risky and therefore is rare. Some rich countries, not least in Western Europe, begin to notice the competition from developing countries. The rich countries continue to exploit the poor countries economically and otherwise, note Cohen (2006). Globalization creates a shared grammar for talking about differences and inequalities.

Cavanagh and Mader (2002) referred to a number of factors that are identified with the term globalization. These factors are: hyper-growth and exploitation of the environment, privatization of public services, global cultural homogenization, promotion of consumerism, integration of national economies, corporate deregulation, and displacement of traditional nation-states by global corporate bureaucracies.

The present stage of globalization is re-described as Americanization (rather than Westernization in the broad sense), or 'globalization by Americanization by Hilger (2008). The process of globalization is one-way and uni-directional, which has brought about a fusion between cultures or, even less, the blending of ethnic groups. The imposition of more and more American icons means less and less possibility for direct inter-ethnic encounter and communication among nations. The collapse of state legitimacy has substantially contributed to the spread of ethnic conflict and nationalism all over the world. The resulting sense of cultural insecurity has spread onto a planetary scale, increasingly accompanied by the reassertion of hurt pride and a rise of patriotism which can easily seize anti-American themes, whenever elites chose to use these in order to gain popular consensus, writes Dennis Smith (2006). The present age of globalization has also brought about the empowerment of 'McMafias', according to Glenny (2008). The idea of a 'global civil society' is yet to be translated into a reality since globalization is responsible for the spread of ethnic conflict, patriotism and nationalism.

The process of globalization affects the world in very many ways. The industrial sector has been subjected to commercialization. There is emergence of worldwide production markets and broader access to a range of foreign products for consumers and companies. The financial sector has also been affected by the globalization which has created worldwide financial markets and better access to external financing for borrowers. The economic sector has been widened because of the realization of the goal of global common market, based on the freedom of exchange of goods and capital. The job market has been considerably expanded all over the world since the workers compete in a global market.

Global economic forces quickly establish a hegemony that subjugates other value systems through a process not unlike that of colonization in the past. The political system has been dramatically changed across the globe in the age of globalization which has created a world government. The information sector has commendably grown over a period of time with the advent of fibre optic communications, satellites, and increased availability of telephone and Internet. The English language has become the 'lingua franca' of globalization. The Internet is associated with the process of cultural globalization because it allows interaction and communication between people with very different lifestyles and from very different cultures. The process of globalization has increased the pollution in the name of development. The advent of new categories of consciousness and identities has created a 'world culture'. Studies have revealed the positive and negative impact of globalization on the mankind.

John Rawls has suggested a model that perhaps can be adapted to the global context. He proposes a redefinition of a 'well-ordered society'. Rawls notes that it is no longer likely that a modern society can be unified around basic moral beliefs. He rather sees order being built around a political conception of justice, a conception found at the focal point of an overlapping consensus of reasonable and comprehensive doctrines. He observes: "Citizens think of themselves as free in three respects: first, as having the moral power to form, to revise, and rationally to pursue a conception of the good; second, as being self-authenticating sources of valid claims; and third, as capable of taking responsibility for their ends." The relationship between multi-culturalism and global justice needs to be examined by the advocates of global free market economics.

The scholars have also analyzed the economic globalization which refers to increasing economic interdependence of national economies across the world through a rapid increase in cross-border movement of goods, service, technology and capital. The process of globalization is centred on the diminution of international trade regulations as well as tariffs, taxes, and other impediments that suppresses global trade. The economic globalization is the process of increasing economic integration between countries, leading to the emergence of a global marketplace or a single world market. The economic globalization comprises the globalization of production, markets, competition, technology, and corporations and industries. Studies have reported certain positive financial effects of globalization. Economic globalization is often referred to as 'corporate globalization' because it is primarily the mission of larger corporations to globalize their operations.

Globalization has posed series of threats to cultural, environmental, legal, ethical and developmental spheres of human life even though it is a process which cannot be ignored by the mankind. The national boundaries have often become irrelevant since the market forces have established their supremacy over the administration, development, business and other spheres of human life. The process of globalization has brought about serious imbalances in the distribution of wealth all over the world. The moral and ethical questions of globalization need to be examined by various stakeholders in order to ensure effective checks and balances in the interest of social justice.

Impact of Globalization on World Media

Scholars have defined globalization differently. Some define it as a set of processes changing the nature of human interaction across a wide range of spheres including the economic, political, social, technological, and environmental. Practically, globalization is perceived as the process of integration of the world community into a common system either economic or social. It essentially means the growing increase in the inter-connectedness and inter-dependence among the world's regions, nations, governments, business and institutions. Some others say, it is a process, which engenders free flow of ideas, people, goods, services and capital thereby fostering integration of economies and societies. The most visible aspect of globalization is the spread of information and communication technologies.

Globalization has been defined as a social process in which the constraints of geography on social and cultural arrangements recede and in which people become increasingly aware that they are receding. The traditional constructs of time and space are broken down during the process of globalization, thereby stimulating the renegotiation of societal relationships. Individuals and groups attempt to explain these major shifts and events at local, national, and international levels. The World Bank and the International Monetary Fund have played a major role in the corporate expansion on an international scale in the age of globalization. The early studies revealed that a few Western nations controlled the international flow of information.

Giddens (1999) has described globalization as 'the intensification of worldwide social relations which link distant localities in such a way that local happenings are shaped by events occurring many miles away and *vice versa*'. This process of 'globalization' is often portrayed as a positive force which is unifying widely different societies and cultures integrating them into a 'global village', and enriching all in the process. It is variously described as an inevitable by-product of human evolution and progress, as if it were an organic process, governed by the laws of nature. However, globalization is not necessarily a natural progression emerging out of the ordinary communication and interaction of people and cultures around the world. It results from deliberate human choice by a powerful group of nations, Transnational Corporations (TNCs) and international organizations which have stakes in the process. The new communication and information technologies have provided methods for large corporations to maximize profits by entering foreign markets.

Thomas Friedman (1997) observes: "Globalization is not a choice. It's a reality. There is just one global market today, and the only way you can grow at the speed your people want to grow is by tapping into the global stock and bond markets, by seeking out multinationals to invest in your country and by selling into the global trading system what your factories produce. And the most basic truth about globalization is this: No one is in charge—not George Soros, not the 'Great Powers'."

Scholars have noted that the world has witnessed four phases of the growth and development of international communication. The first phase saw the emergence of development communication as a full-fledged discipline in 1960s. The second phase witnessed the cultural imperialism in 1970s. The third phase saw the acceptance of Mac Bride Commission Report which pleaded for communication balance across the globe in 1980s. The fourth phase saw the globalization of communication services in the age of economic liberalization in 1990s. All these four phases originated mainly due to the big brotherly attitude of USA which has dominated the global economic and media scenario.

The economists have examined the media economics which includes the economic polices and practices of media companies and disciplines including journalism and the news industry, film production, entertainment programmes, print, broadcast, mobile communications, internet, advertising and public relations. Deregulation of media, media ownership and concentration, market share, intellectual property rights, competitive economic strategies, company economics, media tax and other issues are considered parts of the field. Media economics has social, cultural, and economic implications. Regular study of media economic issues began in the 1970s but flourished in the 1980s with the addition of classes on the subject in U.S. and European universities. Prominent among the media economists include—Steven S. Wildman, Alan Albarran, Bruce M. Owen, Ben Compaine, Stuart McFadyen, Gillian Doyle, Karl Erik Gustafsson, Nadine Toussaint Desmoulins, Achour Fenni and Stephen Lacy. The media economics research has grown over a period of time as a systematic discipline all over the world.

The global communication at the turn of the 21st century has brought about many effects and blurred the cultural, political, economic and technological boundaries. The print, electronic and new media technologies have developed fairly independently over a period of time. The new media technologies including the satellite communication are undermining the traditional boundaries and sovereignty of nations. The Direct Broadcast Satellite (DBS) is violating national borders by broadcasting foreign news, entertainment, educational, and advertising programmes with impunity. Similarly, the micro-media of global communication are narrow casting their messages through audio and videocassette recorders, fax machines, computer disks and networks, including the Internet and the World Wide Web. Practically, the new patterns of global communication are creating the new global cultural and economic orders which are strongly supported by global advertising and the entertainment industry.

The phenomenon of media globalization along with the increasing abundance of media-text production has produced various effects which are being researched by communication scholars. Media globalization is a broad topic, which includes television, radio, film, music, the Internet, and other forms of digital media. Media globalization is defined as the phenomenon of expanding multinational corporate media investment, resulting in the emergence of a global oligarchy of first tier corporations, which own and operate a variety of mass media content and distribution technologies including: television, radio, film, music, broadcasting, satellite, telecommunication, cable, newspapers, magazines, publishing companies, Internet content providers, and other forms of converged digital media.

Herman and McChesney (1998) highlight the impact of globalization on media thus: "We regard the primary effect of the globalization process—the crucial feature of globalization and manifestation of the strength of the great powers and TNC's whose interest they serve—to the implantation of the commercial model of communication, its extension to broadcasting and the 'new media' and its gradual intensification under the force of competition and bottom line pressures. The commercial model has its own internal logic and being privately owned and relying on advertiser support, tends to erode the public sphere and to beat a 'cultural entertainment' that is in compatible with a domestic order media outputs are commoditized and designed serve market end, not citizenship needs."

The UNESCO (1978) published the Declaration on Fundamental Principles Concerning the Contribution of the Mass Media which called upon the mass media to contribute effectively to the strengthening of peace and international understanding, to the promotion of human rights, and to the establishment of a more just and equitable international economic order in the world. The media conglomerates are increasingly competing on the international level through foreign investment, mergers, and acquisitions. The merger mania seems to be the rule of the day when it comes to multinational corporations. McChesney noted that sixty or seventy first and second tier multinational corporations control a major portion of the world's media in the areas of publishing, music, broadcasting, television production, cable, satellite distribution, film production, and motion picture theatre exhibition.

MacBride and Roach (2000) reported that media globalization gained further momentum in the 1980s, when a prevailing policy of deregulation of media in many developing nations along with openness to private investment occurred. McChesney (2005) also noted this trend of free-market deregulation occurring in the eighties and the nineties, in the cable and digital satellite systems around the world. Head and McGregor (2001) observed that in the mid-1980s privatization and deregulation gained momentum in Europe, in the cable and telephone industries, through foreign investment. Critics of media globalization have long held that the United States is far too powerful and that it exercises cultural imperialism over smaller nations by overwhelming them with movies and television programmes produced in the United States writes McChesney (2005).

In the age of globalization, media imperialism has been examined by the media scholars seriously across the globe. They have argued that media imperialism follows logically from cultural imperialism. The Western countries have achieved the goal of cultural imperialism through media imperialism which creates the conditions for conformity to the hegemony culture and limits the possibilities of effective resistance to it. These scholars have challenged the US hegemony effectively in a wide variety of ways. The US has the largest media industry by far and its practices are invariably taken to be the state-of-the-art. The capitalist consumerism is equated with the Americanization of capitalism. It implies that if American influence could be excluded then cultural and media imperialism would end. The cultural critics have argued that the media institutions of America have brought about the American cultural imperialism.

Tehranian (1992) notes: "The global communication is empowering hitherto forgotten groups and voices in the international community. Its channels have thus become the arena for contestation of new economic, political, and cultural boundaries. Global communication, particularly in its interactive forms, has created immense new moral spaces for exploring new communities of affinity rather than vicinity. It is thus challenging the traditional top-down economic, political, and cultural systems. In Iran, it facilitated the downfall of a monarchical dictatorship in 1978-79 through the use of cheap transistor audiocassette recorders in conjunction with international telephony to spread the messages of Ayatollah Khomeini to his followers within a few hours of their delivery from his exile in Paris."

Ganley and Ganley (1992) comment: "In the Philippines, the downfall of the Marcos regime in 1986 was televised internationally for all to witness while alternative media were undermining his regime domestically. In Saudi Arabia, a BBC-WGBH programme on 'The Death of a Princess', banned by the Saudi government as subversive, was smuggled into the country by means of video-tapes the day after its premier showing on television in London. In China, despite severe media censorship, the democracy movement in Tiananmen Square spread its message around the world in 1989 *via* the fax machines. In the Soviet Union, computer networkers who opposed the Moscow coup of 1991 and were sympathetic to Yeltsin, transmitted his messages everywhere despite severe censorship of the press and broadcasting."

The Economist (1996) reports: "In Mexico, the Zapatista movement managed to diffuse its messages of protest against the government worldwide in 1994 through the Internet. In this fashion, it solicited international support while embarrassing the Mexican government at a critical moment when it was trying to project a democratic image for admission to the North American Free Trade Agreement (NAFTA). In Burma or Myanmar, as it is officially known, both government and opposition have employed the Internet in their political struggles. E-mail has been used to achieve rapid global mobilization for withdrawal of Western companies from Myanmar in protest against the government's repressive policies."

These instances clearly demonstrate that accelerating technological advances in communication science and technology have brought about remarkable progress in the field of mass communication and journalism. The modern media institutions are profoundly changing the various spheres of human life. They are also facilitating transfers of science, technology, information, and ideas from the centres to the peripheries of power. On the other, they are imposing a new cultural hegemony through the 'soft power', according to Nye and Owens (1996). The new communication technologies have profoundly transformed the nature of human society all over the world and have served as new actors in international relations.

The communication revolution has led to the emergence of a new class system of information haves and have-nots within and among nations. The acquisition of modern science and technology is the key to catching up. In this process, the role of information technologies, from print to the internet, cannot be overemphasized. The impact of global communication on international cultural life is perhaps the most visible of its effects. Through global satellite and computer networks, trans-border data flows, scientific and professional electronic mailing, and commercial advertising, the macromedia are supporting the globalization of national markets, societies, and cultures. The new media are closely interlinked via social networks of governments, markets, and civil societies. Without contextualizing their social and political functions in historically and cultural specific situations, media effects would, therefore, remain largely mystifying and incomprehensible.

Scholars have examined the relationship between media and globalization across the world and noted a variety of effects resulting from media globalization. Some of these observed effects are open to interpretation while others are acknowledged by most communication scholars. Certain researchers tie their observations to their own theories which attempt to explain certain observed effects. The media programmes that contain violent materials are considered to travel well according to Jhully (2009).

Jonas has singled out media technology as one of the major phenomena separating the possibilities of 20th century humanity from those available to the Greeks. In reality, the process of globalization has brought about a new era of 'exclusive development' instead of 'inclusive development'. The media are used as instruments of manipulation by the owners who are basically wedded to *status-quoism*. The new communication technologies have also widened the gap between the haves and havenots. Media are used by the advertisers to manufacture the consent of the people in favour of the goods and services produced by them. In the information revolution age, the media create a profound discontinuity between past and future and widen the gap between the privileged and under-privileged sections of society.

Robert McChesney (2005) criticized multinational corporations in a number of ways. He observed that the global media market is dominated by eight multinational corporations, namely—General Electric, AT and T/Liberty Media, Disney, Time Warner, Sony, News Corporation, Viacom and Seagram and plus Bertelsmann, the Germany-based conglomerate. The scholar also found that international deregulation and free-market policies have created a climate that has been conducive to foreign investment in media. Ferguson (2002) has stated that cultural homogeneity is a myth which is predicated upon McLuhan's theory of a global village. The myth is not evidenced by real-world observation since identical consumer products, movies, clothes and architectural expressions are not seen in every nation.

Theoretical Foundations

Tomlinson (2002) examined several issues related to cultural imperialism discourse and noted that traditional Marxism divided the world into a political-economic dialectic struggle between an elite ruling class and a larger working class. For the Marxist, capitalism is interpreted as a 'homogenizing cultural force'. The scholar observed that capitalism propels a sort of cultural convergence which people are not able to resist and that cultural imperialism implies a spreading culture of worldwide consumerism. As a matter of fact, cultural imperialism is used as a term which described a foreign culture invading an indigenous community. Anthropologists and linguists alike have described how the very words and customs that are incorporated into most indigenous cultures and languages are a reflection of the environment in which the people live. Tomlinson visualized cultural imperialism as a critique of modernity.

The Frankfurt School which was founded in 1923 contributed critical theory of communication which continues to be an important methodology in the study of mass communication. According to Littlejohn (2002), the Frankfurt School is well-known for its Marxist traditions. The criticism of the mass media from the Frankfurt School was tied to a harsh critique of capitalism and liberal democracy. Critical theory and cultural imperialism theory share common roots in Marxist ideology, which are both anti-capitalistic and generally anti-Western in their approach to the study of media globalization. Rogers used the term 'critical school' which refers to not only a dozen or so important intellectuals originally affiliated with the Frankfurt school but also to hundreds of other contemporary scholars who consider themselves intellectual descendants of the original Frankfurt scholars.

George Gerbner (1977) has developed cultivation analysis theory which asserts that television has displaced traditional sources of socialization such as: the family, the church, and the school. The scholar observed that the dominant communication agencies produce the message systems that cultivate the dominant image patterns. They structure the public agenda of existence, priorities, values, relationships. They have perceived that mass communication changed the production and distribution of knowledge. According to Gerbner,

Gross, Morgan and Signorielli (1986), television has become the primary common source of socialization and everyday information (mostly in the form of entertainment) of an otherwise heterogeneous population. Gerbner further noted that mass media produced images from the mainstream of a common symbolic environment.

Signorielli (1990) noted that heavy television viewers are more prone to be mistrustful of others and to see the world as a meaner place, than do lighter television viewers. Signorielli and Morgan (1990) observed that television makes a small but significant contribution to heavy viewers' beliefs about the world. The cultivation research is concerned with the most general consequences of long-term exposure to centrally-produced and commercially supported systems of stories. Another scholar Noelle-Neumann contributed a spiral of silence theory which proposed that people are more likely to publicly express their opinions when they perceive that others share their views. The spiral of silence effect refers to individuals choosing to be silent when faced with the potential of criticism by others.

Oliver Boyd-Barrett and Terhi Rantanen (2002) discussed the roots of dependency theory which arose from South American nations in the post-colonial stage. It maintained that in the past, colonial nations had been exposed to North American capitalistic investment and became dependent upon western news agencies since the news-system provided a critical link between the developing nations and the larger world economy and corresponding value system. Dependency theory had an impact as part of the non-aligned nation's movement which called for even distribution of communication resources and services across the globe.

Bloch and Lemish (2003) coined a new term, namely megaphone effect which suggests a two-step process. First, cultural texts cross the Atlantic (or Pacific) and enter into the culture of the United States. The second step occurs when these texts are then perceived as having wider international appeal, and are then marketed and distributed to the global community. The scholars examined television programmes, news networks, children's culture and pop music and noted that the adoption of local cultural texts into mainstream U.S. culture provided a greater opportunity for their voices to be heard on a global scale.

O'Neill (1993) built a strong case for a more homogenized world culture and noted that communications technology always influences human organization. His work viewed media globalization from the point of view of a news reporter. Winston Churchill was opposed to using television but later conceded to its necessity. O'Neill attributed Margaret Thatcher's rise to political power as stemming from her television appearances in the 1974 election. The scholar strongly argued that mass communication, on a global scale, drives public opinion. O'Neill's view of communication technology as a major force behind human organizations and political movements is similar to Marshall McLuhan's theory of technological determinism.

Marshall McLuhan and Bruce Power (1989) contributed the Tetrad Theory which is made up of three elements. The first element is visual space which refers to a Western civilization mind set, based on logical systematic, linear, and Platonic reason. The second element is acoustic space, which is more holistic and Asian in approach. The third element is the tetrad itself which is a collision of these two opposing philosophies in a four part metaphor, consisting of enhancement, reversal, retrieval and obsolescence. The study dealt with the invention of the automobile which greatly aided the need for transportation, but also changed society by transforming workers into distance commuters. Gordon Gow (2001) has written an article about tetrad theory and relates it to special metaphor, from an ontological perspective. This approach is used as a model for the study of culture and technology. In this sense, tetrad theory is more of an epistemological perspective than a methodological approach to global mass media research.

Head, Spann and McGregor (2001) examined the effects of media and noted that media institutions performed the role of gate keeping and agenda setting. They observed that mass media organizations are seeking new sources of media content for global distribution. In the age of media convergence, a higher percentage of media-texts and contents are reduced to the digital domain. Joseph Dominick (2002) pointed out that the new media of communication facilitated not one-to-many but rather, many-to-many communication services to the mankind in the age of globalization. The study also revealed that users have simultaneously become producers and consumers in the age of Internet Revolution.

Pavlik and McIntosh (2005) contributed a theory of media globalization called 'Interactive Global Media Theory' which pointed out that feedback in the converged world of digital communication is instantaneous in comparison with traditional analogue mass communication. The study further revealed that television has become an increasingly interactive medium of communication which is accessible to millions of viewers all over the world. The scholars noted that cable television currently has interactive capabilities allowing viewers to order a pizza directly through the cable connection. Third, there is an increasing competitive pressure between first tier multinational media corporations to offer more locally produced content.

Scholars have discussed the subject of globalization from the perspective of the media management and pointed out that media globalization has aided in both the production and distribution of information. The phenomenon of media globalization along with the increasing abundance of media-text production has produced various effects which are being researched by communication scholars. Studies have revealed that major global media corporations have achieved monopoly over media institutions. The phenomenal expansion of multinational corporate media investment has resulted in the emergence of a global oligarchy of first tier corporations, which own and operate a variety of mass media content and distribution technologies including: television, radio, film, music, broadcasting, satellite, telecommunication, cable, newspapers, magazines, publishing companies, Internet content providers, and other forms of converged digital media.

Globalization of media is not a term of global nature. Sparks (2000) has examined the globalization of communication and noted that global media's audience is too small, too rich and too English-speaking to be considered inclusive. There is little evidence that supports the existence of a global public sphere and the public sphere remains largely state-oriented. There is no question that all these globalizing trends are made possible with the help of mass media at both the domestic and international level, according to the scholar. In reality, globalization is not necessarily a natural progression emerging out of the ordinary communication and interaction of people and cultures around the world. It has practically resulted from deliberate human choice by a powerful group of nations, Transnational Corporations (TNCs) and international organizations which have stakes in the process.

In the age of globalization of media, the world is becoming a much more integrated market based in capitalist or marketplace economics.

The media institutions are subjected to commercialization supported by advertising industry. Roland Robertson (1992) calls such combination global-local productions done with global forms and ideas. Barnet and Cavanagh (1994) present a quantitative assessment of the webs of international finance, telecommunication and trade. The global structure is described in terms of three types of nations, i.e. the core, the semi-periphery and the periphery. Semi-peripheral countries are seen in engaging both in core-like activities (as exploiter) and peripheral-like activities (as the exploited). International transaction data (consumer transactions based on credit card purchases and bank-to-bank exchanges). The semi-peripheral-countries are mainly East Asian countries which are not integrated into the global economy. A comparison of international monetary, telecommunications and trade networks suggests that these three networks are quite similar. GNP per capita was significantly correlated with centrality for all three networks.

Today American media play a prominent role in the global scene. A handful of firms dominate the globalize part of the media system. They include—AOL, Time Warner (U.S.), Disney (U.S.), Vivendi-Universal (French), Bertelsmann (German), Viacom (U.S.), and Rupert Murdoch's News Corporation (Australian). The other four main global firms are AT&T (U.S.), Microsoft (U.S.), and two media groups that are part of much large industrial corporations: General Electric/NBC (U.S.) and Sony/Columbia/TriStar (Japanese) (Variety, 2002). Of the top 10 global media firms, six are American (counting News Corporations as Australian), mostly produce, distribute, and regulate almost all media outlets. These types of companies were growing and globalizing quickly. Time Warner and Disney generated considerable revenue outside of the United States in 2010.

Griffin and Masters (1997) observe: "Some media industries such as the Hollywood films and TV studios represented by the Motion Picture Association of America have long been global in their operation and scope. They control a number of companies in other countries which distributed and exhibited (in theatres) the films they produced in the United Sates. More recently, the owner of Hollywood itself has become globalize, as we have seen. The resulting operation has been scrutinized by critics to see whether the kinds of films produced by Sony will now reflect Japanese rather than American sensibilities."

Straubhaar and La Rose (2004) have observed that global media force competitors to react to them. The other major aspect of globalization is the increasingly worldwide penetration of media technologies which have brought about a new age of interactive communication. The process of globalization is reshaping the world's social, political, economic, and cultural landscapes.

In the age of globalization, several media organizations have come into existence in order to deliver the goods and services to the global audience. Global standard bodies such as the International Telecommunications Union (ITU) allocate satellite orbits, determine broadcast frequencies, and define the standards for telephones, mobile phones, faxes, and Internet connections. Global telecom companies, like Cable and Wireless, run much of the world's communications infrastructure of optical fibre cables, satellite, and high-speed lines. Global media also force competitors to react to them. When Murdoch's Star TV started broadcasting in India, the state television broadcast had to respond with more competitive entertainment or lose its audience.

The other major aspect of globalization is the increasingly worldwide penetration of media technology. Globalization is commonly used as a shorthand way of describing the spread and connectedness of production, communication and technologies across the world. That spread has involved the interlacing of economic and cultural activity. The speed of communication and exchange, the complexity and size of the networks involved, and the sheer volume of trade, interaction and risk give what we now label as 'globalization' a peculiar force. With increased economic interconnection has come deep-seated political changes—poorer, 'peripheral', countries have become even more dependent on activities in 'central' economies such as the USA where capital and technical expertise tend to be located. There has also been a shift in power away from the nation state and towards, some argue, multinational corporations.

Empirical studies are conducted all over the world in order to understand the effects of media globalization. The researchers tie their observations to their own theories which attempt to explain certain observed effects. In contrast, other researchers may take on a more descriptive approach preferring to describe detailed effects and apply the theories of other scholars as models for explanation. Gerbner (1985) stated that the most successful television programmes are no longer made for national consumption but rather for international distribution. He has also noted that media contents are affected by the desire to increase the marketability of international television programmes distribution.

The second tier of media conglomerates are also competing on the international level through foreign investment, mergers and acquisitions. They are mostly based in North America, Western Europe and Japan. Prominent among them include—Dow Jones, Gannett, Knight-Ridder, Hearst, and Advance Publications, Kirch Group, Havas, Media-set, Hachette, Pisa, Canal Plus, Pearson, Reuters and Reed Elsevier. McChesney (2005) observed that sixty or seventy-first and second tier multinational corporations control a major portion of the world's media in the areas of publishing, music, broadcasting, television production, cable, satellite distribution, film production, and motion picture theatre exhibition. The scholar concluded that the effect of the spread of multinational media corporations has resulted in cultural imperialism, a loss of local cultural identity.

Studies have also reported that global media adversely affect local culture, value system and public interest because of increasing media monopoly and imperialism. The scholars have recommended that the public would be better served by stricter regulation of the media. The causes and effects of media globalization will continue to be both observed and debated by communication scholars, sociologists, economists and politicians alike. The trend of continuing media globalization has showed no recent signs of retreat. Both critics and advocates of media globalization agree that there is fierce competition taking place between the first and second tier corporations. The smaller regional second tier corporations don't want to loose market share to the larger multinational corporations. Experience reveals that globalization occurs as a result of the activities in advanced countries of news and entertainment media that produce different programmes. A small number of media conglomerates, based in a few Western countries, dominate the production and global distribution of film, television, popular music, and book publishing. The biggest intentional issue in communication is cultural imperialism which deals with the consequences of media flow across the globe.

In the present times, the liberal capitalism appears to have triumphed to put an end to the history of ideological contestations. The hegemonic state-corporate system will continue to be challenged by sporadic but persistent acts of resistance unless the world learns to respect and celebrate diversity by devolutions of power to sub-communities of a national entity. Huntington (1993) argues: "A clash of civilizations is characterizing our own era because new economic and communication power is enabling the ancient civilizations of Asia to challenge the truth claims of the relatively new nations of Europe and America. However, thanks to global communication, a new dialogue of civilizations is also being conducted *via* the international communication networks. Communication technologies are enabling the past silent voices to be heard in a global Tower of Babel characterized by old and new ethnic and racial hatreds. But global communication networks are also fostering a new ecumenicalism leading to the negotiation of new global worldviews and ethics.

Today, the central task of the media in democratic societies may be considered to be two-fold: (1) to allow for the diversity of voices in society to be heard, and (2) to channel that diversity into a process of democratic integration of public opinion and political will formation. Scholars have argued that without free and vigorous debate among competing views, no nation can achieve the level of integrated unity and determination necessary for democratic societies to act on public issues. Studies have reported that media pluralism would serve these purposes better than a media system exclusively dominated by state, commercial, public, or community media. Pluralism in structures of ownership and control are, therefore, needed in order to obtain pluralism in perspectives and messages. However, structural pluralism is hostage to the presence of independent market institutions and voluntary associations (political parties, trade unions, religious and civic organizations). The existence of a strong civil society to counter the powers of the state and the market is, therefore, a precondition for media pluralism.

The media institutions are operating in three markets, namely—market for creative content, market for financial resources and market for manufacturing the consent of the customers. The power of media has grown commendably over a period of time but the media power is not directed at creating a just society since it has the ability to act in pursuit of one's aims and interests, the ability to intervene in the course of events and to affect their outcome, according to Thomas

(2000). There are several empirical evidences which demonstrate that American and European media institutions dominate the present global media scenario and that the dominant strain of global popular culture remains centred in the West and it always speaks in its own language. The major media houses have also promoted cultural imperialism and uneven distribution of communication services and resources across the globe. Some consequences of media flow are indeed deadly serious and pose serious threats to local culture and society. Media critics have expressed serious concern about the economics underlying the flows of media which tend to tie countries into a global economy based on advertising and consumption.

The UN-Sponsored World Summits on the Information Society (WSIS) in Geneva in 2003 and Tunis in 2005 have given a serious thought to the global information and communication order. There is considerable empirical evidence which points to the global concentration of power over media production and distribution in Western nations, states and corporations. In a sense, the global form is localized for the purposes of global capitalist development, expansion of media monopoly and expression of local identity.

The continued dominance of the First world countries over global economy and media under the leadership of the Unites States and Western Europe has posed certain challenges to the developing nations. In the present times, the big corporate organizations dominate the media and related industries in the new millennium. The formulation of locally relevant media policy assumes great significance in the age of globalization since it has a bearing on the structure, conduct and performance of media organizations. The advocates of public interest have strongly questioned the decreasing relevance of nation-state by the media controlled by the market forces. The media globalization presents significant challenges for media and cultural policy.

Impact of Globalization on Print Media in the World

Print media broadly include the newspapers, periodicals, books, professional journals, house journals and other publications which inform, educate and entertain the masses. Print media also advertise the products and services delivered by various organizations. Print media are the oldest form of mass communication in the world. In 1440 the printing press was invented by Johannes Gutenberg. This invention proved itself to be a huge advancement in globalization because it allowed globalization of knowledge. The print media also served the mankind as the fourth estate of democracy in the world. However, the print media are accessible to the literate sections of the society who constitute the minority group.

Theories of Press

The print media became accessible to the people in the world during 16th century. Several scholars have examined the relationship between the government and press. The authoritarian theory of the press evolved in England during the 16th century on the basis of the belief that ruling elite should undertake intellectual exercises in the society. The advocates of authoritarian theory highlighted the press censorship which benefited the ruling class and punished the critics of the government.

In the 17th century, the libertarian theory emphasized that people have the right to information, criticism, participation and progress. The champions of libertarian theory advocated that people are the masters and the rulers should respond to the aspirations of the people. The governments were called upon to serve the people and encourage active people's participation in the process of public opinion formation which is the lifeblood of democracy.

In the 18th century, the social responsibility theory advocated that media institutions are basically public service oriented institutions. The champions of this theory emphasized that media institutions are accountable to the people. The theory holds that the press has a right to criticize the government and function as the voice of the people in a democratic set up. The advocates also upheld that press is the fourth estate of democracy which has the responsibility of serving the society as the watch-dog of public interest.

In the 19th century, the communist theory highlighted that media should be owned by the people who are duly represented by the state. The advocates supported the Marxist system which intends to create an egalitarian system of governance and development. The theory holds that press and other media of communication should function responsibly as the instruments of equality and justice which benefit the working class.

These normative theories of the press are based on certain norms and guidelines which govern the process of journalism. Subsequently, two more theories of communication, namely development theory and participation theory emerged and provided the basis for media functions in the society. The advocates of development theory highlighted that media should function as the instruments of social and economic development. The champions of participation theory advocated that media should facilitate active participation of people in the process of development.

Joseph, R. Dominick (1996) traces the history of the print media thus: "The history of the print media is characterized by political, social, economic and technological developments that have changed the shape of the newspaper, magazine and book industries but, in the final analysis, those publications that have succeeded, persisted and prospered have all been able to attract readers. Many historians suggest that the Chinese first invented movable type and also discovered the process for making paper. Guttenberg provides the only real documentation for naming in father of the printing press. The idea of a mass-circulated newspaper followed the invention of printing. Benjamin Harris published the first American newspaper 'Public Occurrences Both Foreign and Domestic' in 1686. Benjamin Franklin became the publisher of the Pennslyvania Gezette in 1729 which became the most successful colonial newspaper. Newspapers grew in numbers in the period before the Revolutionary War. As America's political relations with England deteriorated, magazines, like newspapers, assumed a more significant political role. Joseph Pulitzer, who edited the New York, World had obviously found a formula for newspaper success, and his innovations are worth considering. The Depression had great social and economic impact on newspapers and magazines. After World War II, economic forces continued to shape the American newspaper, magazine and book industries."

Nature of the Newspaper Industry

In the beginning, journalism functioned as the value-based profession and served the mankind as a prominent instrument of public instruction. Joseph Pulitzer edited 'The New York World' and attracted public attention for editorial independence, human-interest stories, professional excellence and social responsibility. He is widely respected in the world as the founding father of value-based journalism. In India Raja Ram Mohun Roy, Gandhi, Ambedkar, Nehru and other statesmen practiced value based journalism. Thomas Jefferson strongly advocated the freedom of press and upheld that he preferred press without government. Subsequently, business forces entered the field of journalism and converted it into a profitable industry over a period of time.

The modern print media were controlled by the economic forces and the post-war economy forced the newspaper industry to proceed towards consolidation. In 1970s, the newspaper groups owned chains which were in a position to share expenses and generate adequate income. Several factors like ownership, economics, technology, content and so on dominated the print media during 1980s in the world. The print media come under the private monopoly in the world. A minority of the newspapers and periodicals were also brought out by the government agencies. In the 1990s, online newspapers emerged in the digital format and posed serious threat to traditional print media. There is increasing concentration of ownership among the large business houses. There is remarkable growth of newspaper group ownership across the world. Statistically speaking, there are big, medium and small newspapers. A typical newspaper organization has administrative, business, editorial—news, printing and management information departments which play a major role in the production of a newspaper.

Normally, the newspapers earn their revenue from circulation, advertising and job printing sources. Advertising provides more than 75 per cent of revenue to the newspaper through national advertising, local advertising, classified advertising and pre-prints. The advertising revenue is closely related to the circulation status of the newspapers and magazines. The circulation revenue includes all the receipts from selling the paper to the readers. The general expenses of a newspaper organization include—production cost, advertising cost, circulation cost, distribution cost and administrative cost. The structure of newspaper industry is dramatically changing in the age of globalization. The print media are facing tough competition from the electronic and new media in the new millennium. The changing marketing conditions have brought about new ventures in contemporary journalism.

The global news agencies are playing a major role through

consolidation of information networks within and outside national boundaries. They also contribute to internationalization of journalistic services on the basis of improved global communication networks, technologies and operations. These agencies also provide the data which enable the fraternity of journalists to gain the benefit of access to the widest and latest information inputs. These agencies have contributed substantially towards the homogenization of global culture in form and source.

The print media are affected by the process of globalization and the increasing abundance of media-text production has produced various effects which are being researched by communication scholars, observes Dominick (2002). The media globalization is defined as the phenomenon of expanding multinational corporate media investment, resulting in the emergence of a global oligarchy of first tier corporations, which own and operate a variety of mass media content and distribution technologies including: television, radio, film, music, broadcasting, satellite, telecommunication, cable, newspapers, magazines, publishing companies, internet content providers, and other forms of converged digital media. The easy availability of more user-friendly, cost-effective, novel and networked platforms like e-book, reading material on mobile, etc. pose another problem for print media. The emerging social media are also affecting all mainstream media, more so the print media, especially now in the times of global recession.

The print media have undergone series of changes all over the world in the age of globalization. The British press has achieved considerable progress under the private monopoly as the prominent instrument of democracy. The Chinese press has grown enormously under the governmental control as the major instrument of development. The Chinese ownership structure marks the development of a market since there is change of corporate structure which has turned the newspaper industry into a profit-oriented organization. In Egypt, an authoritarian media system is controlled by the government through direct ownership and/or strict media regulations. Besides this, the government of Egypt has also controlled the press which has failed to make its presence felt in the lives of the people.

The press in Australia provides meaningful linkage between democracy and society through free and fair coverage of various issues which enriches the lives of the people. In South Africa, the media ownership is concentrated in the hands of a few corporations. The Constitution Act of 1996 protects and provides for the freedom of the media and access to information in South Africa. The print media industry is relatively open and reflects the country's diversity in respect of languages. The print media is by far the largest sub-sector of media sector in South Africa in terms of the number of titles and ownership.

The print media has been transformed over a period of time in terms of ownership and services all over the world. Series of experiments were made across the globe to change the profile of the journalism and the big newspapers competed with the small newspapers. The trend towards commercialization of press also had considerable impact on the contents of newspapers and magazines. The print media also provided highly diversified contents in order to counter the challenges posed by the modern electronic media. The book industry also grew considerably all over the world. The print media have also become prominent instruments of profit making in the age of globalization. They have also become an essential part of contemporary marketing management process.

In the West, the print media are adversely affected by the remarkable growth and development of electronic media including television and internet. The Economist (2006) claims: "The newspapers are on the way out and that it is only a matter of time before there are closures with half the world's newspapers likely to close in the foreseeable future because business of selling words to readers and selling readers to advertisers, which has sustained their role in society, is falling apart". Another study of Australian newspapers (2006) reported that the reading habits of the people have drastically changed and nearly half of those who read Australian metropolitan newspapers are over fifty. Successful responses to the ubiquitous Internet challenge are essential.

Impact of Globalization on Electronic Media in the World

Basically, the electronic media include—radio, television and the internet. The radio was the prominent medium of electronic communication in the beginning of 20th century. It played a prominent role during the world wars as a medium of political propaganda. In the 1940s, television emerged as the prominent audio-visual medium of communication. It has attracted a vast majority of the people as the most popular and effective medium of mass communication. The Internet has become a prominent means of online communication in the new millennium mainly due to technological revolution.

The electronic media are in the analogue and digital forms which use electronics or electromechanical energy for the end-user (audience) to access the content. The electronic media are subjected to both public and private monopoly usually accompanied by some degree of state regulation which varies from state to state and from cycle to cycle. The public service broadcasting is the commonly found type in all the countries but the private broadcasting system evolved to provide effective competition and opportunities for new and different voices.

Scientists and technocrats played a major role in the second half of the 19th century in facilitating sound recording. Thomas Edition invented phonograph in 1877. Guglielmo Marcony succeeded in sending wireless signal over a two-mile distance. He was responsible for the development of maritime communication which facilitated ship to shore and ship to ship. Fessenden developed the world's first broadcast in 1906 by using a high speed generator. The phonograph, the graphophone and gramophone were developed during 1890s towards establishing recording industry. The radio reached the mass audience by 1920 and played a major role as an instrument of propaganda during the World War I.

Subsequently radio also became a medium of advertisement and generated income for the owners. The radio networks were developed across the world which resulted in the press-radio war. During 1930s, frequency modulated radio was promoted. After the World War II, notable changes took place in the radio and recording industries. The radio broadcasting industry was economically and professionally stabilized during 1955-1970. The radio industry grew remarkably since the rules on ownership were liberalized. The radio stations generated income by selling advertising time and increasing commercial broadcasting services. Radio broadcasting also offered career opportunities to the young generation.

The television also grew as a prominent medium of

communication by 1948. Television posed a serious threat to both print media and radio broadcasting. Television dominated the global mass communication scenario after 1950s on account of technological innovations including the introduction of colour television. Television industry was also expanded all over the world and cable television became very popular in 1960s. The television industry experienced remarkable growth in 1970s. Joseph R. Dominick (1996) writes: "The biggest trend in the TV industry in the 1980s and 1990s was the continuing erosion of the big three network audiences and the increased competition from new networks and cable channels. The world of network broadcasting was shaken by two megadeals, namely the ownership of CapCities/ABC by the Walt Disney Company and buying of CBS by Westing house."

The earlier television started with only a few channels, showing cable, but today there are over 200 channels screening 200 different things. The audience can view channels from across the nation which helps them to understand new lifestyles and cultures of the westernized nations. The television has proved to be a very effective form for entertainment, advertising, sharing cross cultural values and educating the people on several aspects of human life. In the age of globalization, the public and private radio and television channels are competing for attention and income generation. The most ardent of advocates of a private sector recognize a retained and important civic function for public service broadcasting. The market forces are also guided by the economics of broadcasting and the economic rationale favours the increasing ownership concentration.

The most popularly known electronic media today are radio, television and the internet. The radio was a very powerful medium in the beginning but it has lost popularity over a period of time due to certain limitations. Television gained great importance all over the world in all kinds of communities and societies due to its inbuilt characteristics and advantages as an audio-visual medium of communication. It has become the most powerful medium of mass communication throughout the world mainly due to several factors including the globalization.

According to McChesney (2005), the ownership, management and control of electronic media by the major transnational corporations made a big difference. Since they enjoyed absolute financial resources.

The trend of free-market deregulation which occurred in the nineties in the cable and digital satellite systems around the world also paved the way for greater popularity of the electronic media. George Gerbner observed that the most successful television programmes are no longer made for national consumption but rather for international distribution. Gerbner further noted that content is affected by the desire to increase the marketability of international television programme distribution. Programmes that contain violent material are considered to 'travel well' according to Gerbner.

The entertainment and advertisement centred broadcasting services have become very popular in modern society. The media conglomerates are also competing intensely at the global level through foreign direct investment, mergers and acquisitions. Most of the transnational corporations are based in North America, Western Europe, China and Japan. Prominent among them include Dow Jones, Gannett, Knight-Ridder, Hearst, and Advance Publications, and among those from Europe are the Kirch Group, Havas, Media-set, Hachette, Pisa, Canal Plus, Pearson, Reuters and Reed Elsevier. McChesney noted that sixty or seventy-first and second tier multinational corporations control a major portion of the world's media in the areas of publishing, music, broadcasting, television production, cable, satellite distribution, film production, and motion picture theatre exhibition.

The radio and television became the prominent media of communication in the first half of the 20th century since they received large number of listeners and viewers. The audio-video effects became more attractive for the consumers of electronic media since they cut across the barrier of literacy. The advertising industry also used radio and television as prominent means of commercial broadcasting since they had the advantage of video and audio facilities. The value for the advertising slot on television or radio is proportional to the number of viewers or listeners. The electronic media institutions belong to both public and private monopoly all over the world. In case of public control, the electronic media cannot function without the permission or consent of the state. In case of private media the governors of the system enjoy substantial autonomy. But the state regulations control both public and private electronic media all over the world. In reality, the market is the main arena for mass media development and that public service broadcasting is designed to compensate for 'market failure'.

Scholars have also pointed out that increasing growth of multinational media corporations has resulted in cultural imperialism, a loss of local cultural identity. According to McChesney, "The global commercial-media system is radical in that it will respect no tradition or custom, on balance, if it stands in the way of profits." In reality, the United States has emerged as the dominant global media power in the neo-liberal global economic order. The market domination of the media has been most extensive and complete in USA. The Hollywood continues to be the traditional producer and exporter of television programmes in the world. The newly formed secondary television circuits producing local, culturally specific programming are posing serious threat to the Hollywood in the changed circumstances. The international mass media systems which are controlled by the market forces generally affect people's social experiences according to the empirical evidence.

Robertson (1995) states that the local adaptation of an increasingly global form of television illustrates that 'the concept of globalization has involved the simultaneity of what are conventionally called the global and local'. In fact, global diffusion of certain elements of consumer concern by the Western media becomes more effective when those consumer elements are cast in local terms and adapted to local economic conditions.

The cable and satellite television industry has been expanded all over the world due to innovative technologies like Direct Broadcasting Satellite (DBS) or Direct-to-Home (DTH) which started in Japan and Britain. The cable systems and the private satellite TV channels were expanded in Europe, Latin America and Asia. Consequently, a good number of channels became globally accessible and popular over a period of time. They include—CNN, MTV, HBO, ESPN, TNT, Nickelodeon, the Cartoon Network, Discovery, Disney, and other organizations. These channels also broadcast the programmes which fit into the local languages and cultures of Asia, Africa, Latin America and other continents according to Straubhaar and LaRose (2004).

The satellite television service in the world also targeted more specific markets such as India, Taiwan, China, South Asia, Indonesia and Japan, with more localized programming. These channels also found good number of receivers in Latin America and the Middle East regions. Many countries also developed their own satellite television channels which aimed both at national audiences and neighbours within the same cultural linguistic markets. In the new millennium, the digital television and cable TV have become very popular since they provide two-way communication services to the mankind through broadband information services to almost all residents.

The United States is the prominent producer and exporter of television programming in the world. According to the latest statistics, the U.S. television programming accounted for 50 per cent of all broadcasting hours, in the world. In particular, the Hollywood television programming has dominated the global broadcasting scenario and attracted severe criticism from the scholars for cultural empiricism. Scholars have reported that the import of American programming combined with commercial stations, satellite services and cable networks proved to be tremendous tools for accumulating funds for a second phase of active local production. This development has motivated dozens of local television outlets in Europe during the 80s to launch competitive broadcasting services.

New broadcasting technologies such as Direct Broadcasting Satellite (DBS) or Direct-to-Home (DTH) have added a new dimension to electronic media management in the world. Other prominent stakeholders of broadcasting services include Japan and some European countries which operate broadcast digital television services since 1990s. The Eastern European nations have also successfully competed with other nations in providing popular television services according to Television Business International (1997). Studies have reported that the impact of both Hollywood and secondary circuits on the process of globalization is through the dialectic of convergence and divergence. There is evidence of a convergence of organizational structuring in the local, secondary networks production and distribution of tele-novels which have attracted the attention of the world.

In the decade of 1990s, private satellite TV channels blossomed in Europe, Latin America, and Asia. A number of channels quickly became global in reach. Prominent among them include—CNN, MTV, HBO, ESPN, TNT, Nickelodeon, the Cartoon Network, Discovery, Disney, and so on. These private channels have also succeeded in translating and adopting the U.S. channels to the languages and cultures of the new audiences, observe Straubhaar and La Rose (2004).

The private television channels have widened their reach across the globe. The Star TV owned by Rupert Murdoch, originally targeted the whole of Asia with American (MTV, film), European (BBC, sports), and Chinese-language channels. There is consistent expansion of satellite and cable television networks and operations in Latin America and the Middle East.

Antola and Rogers (1984) noted that the Mexican network Televisa accounted for about 50 per cent of all broadcasting hours. Tracey and Redal (1991) have discussed the 'domestic populism' concept which emphasizes the process whereby television is informed by local cultural preferences. All of these theories emphasize that television programming does not necessarily reflect life as a mirror, nor does it superimpose ideology. Rather, its role is constitutive of forming local identities. The studies carried out by Margolis (1996) and de Melo (1995) have also revealed that media convergence imposed a homogenous taste onto larger, more diverse audiences across the globe.

The American model of broadcasting has been generalized and adapted in a global model for commercial media. In some countries, the process of adaptation of global genres or formats is more formally. People have witnessed the scenario of 'cultural dumping' of obsolete American television programmes on a powerless nation-state on the periphery which is an adverse impact. The electronic media also produce various forms of hybridization which conveys the meanings externally originating from images reflecting re-worked, synchronized and blended with existing cultural traditions and forms of life. The creation of the global electronic networks is largely facilitated through the privatization of electronic media, liberalization of electronic markets and deregulation of tariff structures.

The electronic media have not designed the broadcasting services which would benefit the audience in the developing countries. The television channels owned by the western market forces have ignored the local culture and aspirations. The privatization of broadcasting, deregulation, commercialization and consumerism have become the potential threats to cultural and ideological plurality including the national and local identities. The global conglomerates make use of the electronic media to manufacture the consent of the people and create global consumers. The large broadcasters are increasingly marketing their products to smaller broadcasters around the world. The local audiences do not fit into the broadcasting services offered by the electronic media in the age of globalization.

According to Arnander (2004), the wholesale/retail distinction may become less significant as all players offer their news products directly to subscribing computer users, the form of (multi) media consumption predicted to eventually displace television. Despite the increasing number of news services, ownership is highly concentrated, and broadcasters are becoming increasingly depended upon a few news providers to supply the international images they use on the air, to shape our global reality.

The satellite services and cable networks proved to be tremendous tools for accumulating funds for a second phase of active local production through the divergence from the traditional paradigm of Hollywood domination even though the localized producers resisted the monopoly of Hollywood and other multi-national media corporations. Some countries have broken the Western monopoly through locally relevant electronic media programmes. The breaking of the electronic neo-colonialism took place in some Eastern European, African and Latin American countries. The rate of export growth for the producers in developing countries is quite impressive according to the observations of media scholars.

The media convergence has also brought about the globalization of culture over a period of time. The electronic media have facilitated the process of globalization of information, knowledge, entertainment, economy and culture. Scholars have also strongly criticized the proprietary pull of cultural identifications, traditional values and conventional practices to social life in their writings. Experience reveals that neither the convergence nor the divergence perspective alone can adequately account for the complex organizational processes of globalization.

In reality, language and culture play an important role in the media cross borders since the people tend to look for television programming, internet, sites, and music that are culturally proximate. The present generation of media consumers tends to choose media from their own culture or similar culture. The language is a crucial divider of media markets according to Wildman and Siwek (1988). The language certainly shapes music and internet patterns as well. The cultural proximity is a strong factor since the audiences in many countries respond very well to some kinds of imported programmes since the cultural-linguistic markets are emerging at a level smaller than global but larger than national.

Impact of Globalization on Film Media in the World

Film is a prominent medium of communication in the world. A film is also called a movie or motion picture which is a series of still or moving images. A film is produced by recording photographic images with cameras, or by creating images using animation techniques or visual effects. The origin of the name 'film' comes from the fact that photographic film (also called film stock) has historically been the primary medium for recording and displaying motion pictures. Many other terms exist for an individual motion picture, including picture, picture show, moving picture, photo-play and flick.

A common name for film in the world is movie and the additional terms for the profession or industry in general include the big screen, the silver screen, the cinema and the movies. Although the words 'film' and 'movie' are sometimes used interchangeably, 'film' is more often used when considering artistic, theoretical, or technical aspects, as studies in a university class and 'movies' more often refers to entertainment or commercial aspects, as where to go for fun on a date. Film is a combination of art and creativity and attracts the audience in a dramatic manner. The act of making a film is also considered as a work of art. A film basically entertains the audience and generates income for the producer who makes investment in film making. There are several kinds of films.

Basically, film production, distribution, exhibition and publicity activities are very expensive when compared to other kinds of media services. There are various stages of film production which include conception, planning, execution, revision, distribution, publicity and so on. Basically, the important stages of film production include—concept development, mobilization of financial resources, human resources management, pre-production, production, post-production and distribution. The process of film-making has developed into an art form and industry.

Films are cultural artifacts created by specific cultures, which reflect those cultures, and, in turn, affect them. Film is considered to be an important art form, a source of popular entertainment and a powerful method for educating—or indoctrinating—citizens. The visual elements of cinema give motion pictures a universal power of communication. The Vitascope was invented by Thomas Edison in 1896. It projected moving pictures onto a large screen which enabled the masses to see a twenty-by-twelve-foot screen in the middle of the stage. The audiences were thrilled by seeing the motion pictures which fascinated the people. Reynaud was the first person who projected his drawings onto a large screen in 1880s by combining the Zoetrope with a primitive slide projector. Louis Daguerre invented a photographic process that used burnished metal as a base and facilitated the display of clear and detailed photographs.

In 1889, Dickson had perfected the Kinetoscope which showed the films to the audience. Several technologies such as photography (1830s), negative pictures and printing positives (1880s), roll-films (1850s), celluloid (1868), high-sensitivity photographic emulsion (late 1880s), projection (1645) and movement dissection/persistence of vision (1872) enriched the process of film-making. In 1894, the Lumiere brothers developed the innovative means of projecting the motion pictures. The film became a very effective audio-visual means of communication by 1910.

Joel Mokyr (1990) observed that film was an international process of invention, taking place in several countries at the same time, and the inventors building upon and improving upon each other's inventions. This connects to notion that in the nineteenth century communication became increasingly important to innovations, and many innovations depended on international communication between inventors. The film was recognized as a typical nineteenth century invention since it was a smart combination of many existing technologies. Many different innovations in the technologies which it combined had been necessary to make possible the innovation of cinema. Third, cinema was a major innovation in the sense that it was quickly and universally adopted throughout the western world, quicker than the steam engine, the railroad or the steamship.

The film replaced the traditional theatre which entertained the people for several centuries. The film became a prominent means of communication which attracted the global attention. The film industry became the fourth-largest export industry before the World War I. Subsequently, it became the tenth most profitable industry in the world according to Bakker (2001).The film industry grew well in the world after the introduction of sound effects and narrations in 1920s. The production of sound films became very expensive on account of new equipments, technicians, talents and operations. The camera and microphone were moved together in the early talkies.

Kraft (1996) pointed out that in economic terms, sound represented an exogenous jump in sunk costs (and product quality) which did not affect the basic industry structure very much: The industry structure was highly concentrated before sound and the European, New York/Jersey and Florida film industries were shattered. What it did was to industrialize away most of the musicians and entertainers that had complemented the silent films with sound and entertainment, especially those working in the smaller cinemas. This led to massive unemployment among musicians."

Bakker (2005) observes: "The emerging Hollywood studios benefited from first mover advantages in feature film production. They owned international distribution networks. They could offer cinemas large portfolios of films at a discount (block-booking), sometimes before they were even made (blind-bidding), the quality gap with European features was so large it would be difficult to close in one go, and, finally, the American origin of the feature films in the 1910s had established U.S. films as a kind of brand, leaving consumers with high switching costs to try out films from other national origins. It would be extremely costly for European companies to re-enter international distribution, produce large portfolios, jump-start film quality, and establish a new brand of films—all at the same time. The large existing American Northeast coast film industry and the newly emerging film industry in Florida declined as U.S. film companies started to locate in Southern California. The Hollywood also attracted new creative inputs through non-monetary means: even more than money creative inputs wanted to maximize fame and professional recognition."

The film became an important mass entertainment industry during 1930s. The film industry also grew substantially in the U.S., Britain and France. There was a phenomenal growth of film industry since it demanded adequate capital and labour. The film technology also made the entertainment industry a viable endeavour economically and otherwise. It became a well-developed and competitive entertainment industry by 1940s. The resulting national consumer surpluses for entertainment varied from about a fifth of total entertainment expenditure in the U.S., to about half in Britain and as much as three quarters in France. It was also confirmed that film industry made a substantial contribution for the national GDP of a country.

During 1930-1950, studios were established in America, Europe and other parts of the world. The musical films also became very popular. The entertainment oriented films were popular in the beginning. Several directors also produced mythological, historical, social and patriotic films. The studio system was built around financial investment and economics of film making. The governments also enacted various film censorship regulations in order to safeguard the public interest. The star system was also introduced later on. There was a close relationship between the film and television and the television movies were shown on the network television. The film industry generated adequate income since the films were produced on the basis of box office economics which was based on market research. The films appeal to audience segments other than teenagers according to Joseph R. Dominick (1996).

There was vertical disintegration of the Hollywood film industry since production, distribution and exhibition became separate activities that were not always owned by the same organization. Three main causes brought about the vertical disintegration in America. Besides this, certain changes in the social-demographic structure in the U.S. brought about a shift towards entertainment within the Hollywood. The television broadcasting also constituted a new distribution channel for audiovisual entertainment in modern society according to Gomary (1995).

The popularity of television as a prominent means of communication also led to a sharp fall in real box office revenue during 1960-1990. There were more movie screens in the modern society. The proliferation of screens, coinciding with declining capacity per screen, facilitated market segmentation. The vertical disintegration occurred at three levels, namely—the Hollywood studios divested their cinema-chains, they outsourced part of their film production and most of their production factors to independent companies. There were some visible changes in the film industry. Storper and Christopherson (1989) identify certain factors such as replacement of production by a few large companies to many small flexibly specialized companies, emergence of Southern California as an industrial district for the film industry and an intricate network of the businesses, from set design companies and costume makers, to special effects firms and equipment rental outfits.

Bakker (2004) comments on the economics of film-making thus: "Because film production costs were mainly fixed and sunk, international sales or distribution were important, because these were additional sales without much additional cost to the producer; the film itself had already been made. Films had special characteristics that necessitated international sales. Because, they essentially were copyrights rather than physical products, theoretically, the costs of additional sales were zero. Film production involved high endogenous sunk costs, recouped through renting the copyright to the film. The marginal foreign revenue equalled marginal net revenue (and marginal profits after the film's production costs had been fully amortized). All companies large or small had to take into account foreign sales when setting film budgets. Films were intermediate products sold to foreign distributors and cinemas. While the rent paid varied depending on perceived quality and general conditions of supply and demand, the ticket price paid by consumers generally did not vary."

Bakker (2001) further notes: "The films also became branded products since the film producers borrowed branding techniques from other consumer goods' industries in order to secure the audiences. The short product-life-cycle forced them to extend the brand beyond one product—using trademarks or stars—to buy existing 'brands,' such as famous plays or novels, and to deepen the product-life-cycle by licensing their brands. The main value of stars and stories lay not in their ability to predict successes, but in their services as giant 'publicity machines' which optimized advertising effectiveness by rapidly amassing high levels of brand-awareness. After a film's release, information such as word-of-mouth and reviews would affect its success. The young age at which stars reached their peak, and the disproportionate income distribution even among the superstars, confirm that stars were paid for their ability to generate publicity. Likewise, because 'stories' were paid several times as much as original screenplays, they were at least partially bought for their popular appeal."

The blockbuster movie increased cinema attendance since it was heavily marketed and supported by intensive television advertisement. The U.S. film industry received several kinds of tax breaks from the early 1970s onwards. The coinciding with the blockbuster movie and tax-breaks film budgets increased substantially which resulted in a higher perceived quality and higher quality difference with television. There was remarkable rise in multiplex cinemas, cinemas with several screens, increased consumer choice and increase in the appeal of cinema by offering more variety within a specific cinema. Certain changes and developments made the modern film industry change-oriented during 1980s.

During the 1990s the film industries grew substantially in Asia, Africa, Latin America, Middle East, Australia and other regions. The European Union started a large scale subsidy programme for its audiovisual film industry. This seventy-fold difference in performance is remarkable. Even when measured in gross return on investment or gross margin, the U.S. still had a five-fold and two-fold lead over Europe respectively, reports Dale (1990). During the 1990s, the film industry moved into television broadcasting. In Europe, broadcasters often co-funded small-scale boutique film production. In the U.S., the Hollywood studios started to merge with broadcasters.

The commercial films were produced in large number since they competed with the television broadcasting and generated income to the producers. In the 1990s, the structure of the motion picture industry became different. Many hit films were produced since the film industry was based on profit considerations. The organization of the film industry primarily consisted of production, distribution, publicity and exhibition. The films were produced by economically sound individuals and organizations. The distribution network was also developed with a view to supply the prints of films to various theatres. The publicity was carried out extensively in order to attract the attention of audiences. The exhibition segment was controlled by large chain owners. The domestic and foreign companies became very active as film producers.

In the decade of 1990s, several technological developments enriched and diversified the process of film-making. The development of DVD players, home theatre amplification systems with surround sound and subwoofers, and large LCD or plasma screens enabled people to select and view films at home with greatly improved audio and visual reproduction. These new technologies provided a new dimension to audio and visual aspects of film-making. In the new millennium, film-making practically moved towards digital screens, a new approach which allows for easier and quicker distribution of films (*via* satellite or hard disks). The cinema also faced a tough challenge from home video by the likes of a new high definition (HD) format, Blu-ray, which can provide full HD 1080p video playback at near cinema quality. Video formats also gradually catched up with the resolutions and quality of film-making.

In the new millennium, the process of film-making underwent several changes professionally and economically. There were vertical and horizontal film production activities. In case of vertical production, the parent company owned multiple companies across different stages of film industry. The horizontal film production is known for the ownership of multiple companies by the parent company at the same stage of the film industry. Film became a million dollar industry in the 21st century. In the age of globalization, the governments deregulated the entertainment industries and enabled the entrepreneurs to actively participate in the film business through substantial investments. The film industry also witnessed the commercial, formalized and standardized live entertainment patterns.

The processes of globalization, liberalization, privatization, commercialization and so on changed the profile of the film industry in the new millennium. A new age of live entertainment through process innovations emerged over a period of time. In the present times, the film industry has become the modern world of automated, standardized, tradable mass-entertainment, integrating the national entertainment markets into an international one. The feature film industry became more connected to other entertainment industries, such as videogames, theme parks and musicals. With video game revenues now exceed films' box office revenues.

Impact of Globalization on New Communication Technologies in the World

The development of computer brought about the new age of interactive communication in the world. In the decade of 1990s, developments in hardware and software expanded the communication function of the computer. The Internet is a network of computer networks. The journey from ARPANET to Internet during 1970-2000 was marvelous since the new technologies decentralized the whole system of communication by creating an interconnected web of computer networks. The WWW is part of the Internet that contains multimedia items and hypertext, a means of instantly accessing related information.

The world has witnessed commendable Internet Revolution, knowledge expansion and interactive communication in the age of new information and communication technologies which have opened up entirely new vistas of knowledge revolution all over the world. By definition, Information and Communication Technologies are a diverse set of technological tools and resources to create, disseminate, store, bring value-addition and manage information. Consequent on information revolution, knowledge has become a universal property and a major resource for all round development of the mankind. The technology oriented knowledge networking primarily opened up a new way of interactive communication between government bodies, NGOs, academic and research institutions, and the civil society.

Communication scientists have observed that new communication technologies have brought about the globalization of information, education and allied services in modern society. Communication science and technology have shortened the distance between people all over the world. The new media have radically broken the connection between physical place and social place, making physical location much less significant for our social relationships, observe Croteau and Hoynes (2003).

The new media have also created 'virtual communities' across the globe and transcended the geographical boundaries thus eliminating social restrictions. Howard Rheingold (2000) notes: "People in virtual communities use words on screens to exchange pleasantries and argue, engage in intellectual discourse, conduct commerce, make plans, brainstorm, gossip, feud, fall in love, create a little high art and a lot of idle talk. The new media have the ability to connect like—minded persons worldwide. Manovich and Castells (2001) have argued that whereas mass media corresponded to the logic of industrial mass society, which values conformity over individuality, new media follows the logic of the post-industrial or globalized society whereby 'every citizen' can construct his/her own custom lifestyle and select his/her ideology from a large number of choices.

The World Bank organized a forum called 'Voices of Poor' in order to expand the knowledge and enable the mankind to gain the capacity to acquire and generate knowledge in all its forms, including the recovery and upgrading of traditional knowledge, is perhaps the most important factor in the improvement of human condition, according to Benzason and Sagasti (1995).

The new communication technologies have brought about information explosion and created a number of new choices and opportunities in some of the most vital realms of human endeavour. The scholars have also advocated that the digital divide should be eradicated in order to create knowledgeable people in the world and facilitate active participation of people in the process of development. It has been rightly felt that one of the hallmarks of the information society openness is a crucial ingredient of democracy and good governance. Information and knowledge are at the heart of efforts to strengthen tolerance, mutual understanding and respect for diversity. Undoubtedly, the application of new media would improve the quality of life for the marginalized sections of society in the world.

Truely, information technology is the common denominator that links people, irrespective of caste, class, sex, religion, race or political alignments. Scholars have also examined the role of new media in the empowerment of people across the globe. New communication technologies can be used to impart information and that in turn will lead to motivation, mobilization and action. The communication technologies can also encompass different approaches—welfare, participatory and catalyst approaches with women and weaker sections as change agents in different spheres of human life and development. Modern communication technologies have the potential to bypass several stages and sequences in the process of development, encountered in earlier decades.

During the fag end of the 20th century, 'media convergence' became a reality. It commonly refers to the provision of different kinds of services over the existing communication infrastructure and the enhancement of existing technologies so as to provide a wide variety of new services. Convergence of computing and telecommunications was perceived as one of the most important trends in ICT. Scholars have termed the computer networks in convergence with telecommunications as 'information infrastructures' which are viewed as fundamental and critical bases for the participatory development of the mankind. The convergence of carriage and content, along with imaginative applications opened up tremendous possibilities for delivering a big basket to the consumer empowering them to choose, use and control voice data and images delivered through a common device.

The new communication technologies like personal computers, mobile phones and other Information Communication Technology (ICT) devices, the development of satellite, cable and other networks and increased bandwidth have spawned new forms of distribution through which media and entertainment products and services are made available. The restructuring of the media and entertainment industries and their inclusion is a trend towards an integrated information industry is driven to a large extent by these major developments in technology. The flows are entertainment and education materials and promotional messages are carried by networks such as the internet in order to promote new consumer culture. There is a world-wide trend towards a shift from public service type provision of information and telecommunication services to a competitive environment for the trading of these services to public market operators.

Dennis (1992) noted that the new 'multimedia' process provided not only conventional cable television, but also telecommunications services, computer games and software, home banking and shopping, video on demand and other interactive services. The global corporations have secured control over programming, distribution and transmission systems which have brought about a global media space and market which has benefited the market forces.

The media convergence is based on technological innovations in microelectronics, computers and telecommunications. The digitalization of all kinds of data has been achieved on the basis of their common informational structure. In addition, the development of optical fibre and satellite technology has created the possibility for rapid transmission of increasing amounts of information per second. The development of integrated circuits and the exponentially increasing capacity of microchips have also been crucial for data communication and integrating different kinds of electronic communication. All these factors are responsible for the establishment of the modern 'information society'.

The new media have transformed the lives of the people considerably since the foundations of the information superhighway were laid years ago. This whole system of television, radio, cable, satellites and computer networks, microwave, wireless digital, telephone systems, cellular and mobile radio networks basically enable the transmission of information, data, audiovisual material and communications. Everyday people receive, store, process, display and send a variety of texts, sound and images, including films, television and radio programmes across the country and around the world in this age of information revolution.

According to Walter Durling (1999), the major challenge is to integrate these diverse and disparate elements into a high-speed, interactive, broadband, digital, seamless whole to complete the highway, ensuring that it reaches all parts of the world where it is needed, and is made available to as many people as possible. The streaming technology has brought about the revolution in the way we hear and buy recorded music. The trend towards business based on multimedia convergence lies behind many of the mergers and acquisitions now taking place in the media and entertainment industries. The impact of information communication technologies and the related synergy effects and increased efficiency have influenced the numbers and structure of the workforce and significantly changed working conditions and occupational patterns. The World Bank, UNESCO and other agencies have also envisaged the democratization of information resources and services over a period of time and called upon the national governments to establish social media networks at the grassroots level.

The information technologies have profoundly transformed the nature of economy in modern society. The global television communication networks such as CNN, BBC, and Star TV have added new dimension to the international communication. The global communication networks have created a global civil society and pressure groups which have served as new actors in international business and political relations. The impact of global communication on the world economy is perhaps the most discussed aspect of human life. This impact has reshaped the processes of world production, distribution, trade, development, and financing. The expansion of global transportation and telecommunication networks have enabled the multinational corporations to decentralize their production and distribution networks while seeking higher profits in regions of the world with lower wages, rents, taxes, and government regulation. World trade and financing have also been profoundly affected by the Transborder data flows that facilitate network development and business operations.

The communication science and technology oriented new media have changed the profile of the world economically and otherwise. Modern organizations are combining to service the new multimedia environment through a series of corporate mergers and alliances. Politically, global communication is undermining the traditional boundaries and sovereignties of nations. Direct Broadcast Satellite (DBS) is violating national borders by broadcasting foreign news, entertainment, educational, and advertising programmes with impunity. The micro-media of global communication are narrow casting their messages through audio and video cassette recorders, fax machines, computer disks and networks, including the Internet and the World Wide Web. Global communication, particularly in its interactive forms, has created immense new moral spaces for exploring new communities of affinity rather than vicinity. It is thus challenging the traditional top-down economic, political, and cultural systems.

The impact of global communication on cultural arena is also widely debated across the globe. The technological effects are always socially mediated and constructed. The new media have found their own cultural space in different parts of the world. The new media of communication are acting as agents of globalization. The global satellite and computer networks, trans-border data flows, scientific and professional electronic mailing, and commercial advertising and the macromedia are used by the market forces to facilitate the globalization of national markets, societies, and cultures. Global communication channels can serve the cause of world peace and progress if they are used as effective channels of international and inter-civilizational dialogue. The issues like sovereignty, governance, economy, human rights, civic responsibilities, and media systems have to be examined seriously in order to achieve the goal of globalization of prosperity in modern society.

Impact of Globalization on Folk Media in the World

Folk media are known as the oldest media of communication since they have grown along with the human civilizations all over the world. They primarily include—folk songs, folk dance, folk theatre forms and folk traditions. The folk media are also culture oriented media of communication which have served the mankind for quite a long time before the advent of modern mass media. They are also known as the media of the people, by the people and for the people. The folk media also truly represent the culture of the land and convey the cultural significance to the people in different forms. The new technological advances in telecommunications and their worldwide dissemination are profoundly changing the rules of international relations. On the one hand, they are facilitating transfers of science, technology, information, and ideas from the centers to the peripheries of power. On the other, they are imposing a new cultural hegemony through the 'soft power' (Nye, 1990) of global news, entertainment, and advertising. Globalizing the local and localizing the global are the twin forces blurring traditional national boundaries.

In the age of globalization, the market forces are bent upon bringing in cultural uniformity throughout the world without leaving any scope for diversities in order to fulfil their hidden aspirations. The market forces all over the world also wish to impose the dominant culture and way of life everywhere. The media which are owned, managed and controlled by the imperialist forces wedded to America-led globalization have continuously tried to impose Western culture on the audiences across the globe deliberately. Culturally, the new patterns of global communication are creating a new popular culture of commodity fetishism supported by global advertising and the entertainment industry.

The process of globalization has brought in a global culture which is meant something like the culture of the nation-state, extended to cover the entire world. The people are persuaded to accept the ethnoscapes (brought in by flows of people), technoscapes (the flows of machinery and industry), finanscapes (the flows of money in the currency and stock markets), mediascapes (images and information disseminated by print and electronic media), and ideoscapes (flows of the elements of ideologies) as new ways of life. In the present era of globalization, the concept of culture is undergoing a sea change. The old concept of culture is giving way to a new culture which has institutionalized slavery as a way of life.

McChesney concluded that the effect of the spread of multi-national media corporations has resulted in cultural imperialism, a loss of local cultural identity. The global commercial-media system is radical in that it will respect no tradition or custom, on balance, if it stands in the way of profits. Media have speeded up the connection between cultures and thereby started to erase the boundaries of space, and even more profound boundaries of nations and government ensuring free flow of information and influence. The capitalistic nature of media prevents any revolt against the almost monopolistic position the western world has on globalization via media, and there seem to be no authority that can intervene in this process preventing a monopoly. So however romantic the idea of cultures being brought closer together is, there are also power struggles and the possibility to exploit this development, which American officials openly admit to be attempting.

The year 1998 was a critical stage for the debate on globalization which focused the attention of the scholars on the cultural implications of globalization. Henry Kissinger (1999) observes: "The basic challenge is that what is called 'globalization' is really another name for the dominant role of the United States. During the past decade, the United States has created unprecedented wealth, broadened and deepened the availability of capital; funded the creation, development and broad distribution of a wide variety of new technologies, created markets for an endless array of goods and services... in economic terms it can get no better: full employment, rising real wages, increasing productivity, low inflation, increasing wealth and non-stop growth. ... For America, these are the good old days." The champions of Americanization have also stated that the world had no alternative but to accept American ideas, values and way of life.

Thomas L. Friedman, a foreign affairs columnist of *The New York Times* declares: "We Americans are apostles of the Fast World, the prophets of the free market and high priests of high tech. We want 'enlargement' of both our values and Pizza Huts. We want the world to follow our lead and become democratic and capitalistic, with a Web site in every pot, a Pepsi on every lip, Microsoft Windows in every computer and with everyone, everywhere, pumping their own gas. Globalization has its own dominant culture, which is why it tends to be homogenizing. Culturally speaking, globalization is largely, though not entirely, the spread of Americanization—from Big Macs to Mickey Mouse—on a global scale."

The propagandists also emphasize that the roots of local culture and values which are enshrined in the folk media pose serious threats to the dominance of American culture. Deliberate efforts are made by the media organizations to propagate the American culture which suits America which is the most advanced capitalist society in the world today. The media institutions which are controlled by America led transnational corporations have advocated that globalization is leading to cultural homogeneity. This kind of pernicious propaganda has led to cultural degeneration which is injurious to the health and progress of the people in the rest of the world. The death of folk media spells a disaster to the rest of the world culturally and otherwise.

The Third World Nations are forced to subscribe to the American ideology which has belittled the significance of local culture and folk media over a period of time. The champions of social justice have also persuaded the local citizens not to follow the American model which is responsible for the decline of the human values, ethical norms, democratic aspirations and other considerations for the sustainable culture, environment and development in modern society. The activists have also cautioned the local administrators and citizens against America led globalization which is the direct consequence of Western culture across the planet.

Scholars have also discussed at length the concept of cultural imperialism which represents the use of political and economic power to exalt and spread the values and habits of a foreign culture at the expense of native culture. They have rightly observed that cultural imperialism arises in the world economic system, with the terms and nature of production settled at one location and nurtured elsewhere. The guerilla advertising launched by the multi-national corporations has manufactured the consent of the local people in favour of American imperialism, goods and services. The goods and services also invariably transmit the ideology and values of the world capitalist system dominated by America.

The cultural imperialism also causes a death blow to the local culture and folk media since it increases the demand for the goods and services manufactured by the multi-national corporations by fostering a consumerist mentality. The modern media of communication have posed serious threat to folk media in the age of globalization which has considerably increased the means through which nationals of one country actively take part in another country's cultural, economic and political life.

In the age of globalization, a new 'consumer culture' has emerged on account of planned and deliberate media campaigns which have adversely affected the local culture and influenced the domestic consumption patterns of other societies. Folk media are also losing their significance because of the onslaught of modern mass media which are wedded to globalization led by America and Europe. The new consumer culture implies that both material and non-material items, including kinship, affection, art, and intellect become co-modified. The world has also witnessed the phenomenon of hyper commodification in which minute differences between products or minute improvements in them can determine variations in demand through brand names.

Cronk (1996) has noted that the traditional values of Western society were getting corrupted by commercialization of culture and the impact of mass media. The commercialization of culture and marginalization of folk media have brought about the cultural degeneration and belittlement of traditional media in the age of globalization. The people in other societies have become acclimatized to television, film, internet and other Western media which make the people believe that their being is shaped by what they see in Western media and consume on the basis of Western influence.

The modern media are also known as 'class media' which disseminate information, education, entertainment and advertisement which have become key sources of social differentiation, displacing traditional, cultural, national and political affiliations. The new consumer culture also systematically liberates values and preferences from particular social and geographical locations. It also invalidates the social and political structures of modernity including states. The modern media are used for the purpose of undermining the cultural classifications of modernity, technically by declassifying or dedifferentiating culture according to the empirical evidence. Capitalism has weakened the foundations of local culture, norms, ethics and other values of life which are enshrined in the folk media.

In the age of globalization, English has become the medium of communication. The local languages are also neglected because of the addiction of people to modern media which are English-centred. In the case of folk media, the communication services are delivered in the language of the people which represents their ability to communicate more freely and easily in order to foster greater mutual understanding and appreciation of one another's problems and points of view in a democratic way. The emergence of a virtual paradise on account of technological innovations has threatened balkanization of nation-states in which culture is pitted against culture, people against people, tribe against tribe and media against media.

The protagonists of America-led globalization have worked against cultural promotion, social justice, inclusive development, integrated development, sustainable development, collective welfare and other constitutional obligations and cultural norms. The gap between the rich and poor has widened in the age of globalization. The new 'Occupy Wall Street Movement' has strongly advocated that globalization has rendered redundant the age-old aspiration of nations to strive for economic self-sufficiency. The new advocates have strongly pleaded for the establishment of an egalitarian state which protects local culture, environment, human values, social justice, economic equity and other norms of distributive justice and development in the new millennium.

The folk media forms which have remained as informal universities of the mankind have been precariously placed by the market forces led modern media. Folk media have created lot of awareness among the people about history, culture, environment, human values and so on since times immemorial. In the age of globalization, folk media are withering away because of the increasing popularity of modern media, absence of social intervention, inadequate funding, negligence of people and other factors. These threats and disadvantages have rendered the folk media near-relics in today's business environment.

Scholars have also emphasized the need for cultural promotion and rejuvenation of folk media in order to save the mankind from the exploitative forces led by America in the name of globalization. Several individuals and committees have called upon the government organizations, universities, community organizations, local bodies, non-government organizations and other stakeholders to facilitate meaningful integration of traditional and modern media in order to save the folk media and local culture against the menace of market forces.

Impact of Globalization on Corporate Advertising in the World

The word 'advertising' is derived from its Latin root *adverter,* which means 'to turn towards' or 'to attract attention'. Advertising basically comprises all acts that are directed towards drawing the attention of people about the availability of goods and services. Advertising is commonly defined as any form of non-personal presentation and promotion of ideas, goods and services usually paid for by an identified sponsor or advertiser. Advertising is also directed at a specific group of consumers of goods and services. Advertising is a paid form of communication. The advertiser is also duly identified by the media of advertising for obvious reasons. Advertising has become a necessary evil in the modern society. Advertising has promotional, educative, economic and social dimensions.

Advertising is usually delivered through a communication medium designed to reach more than one person but to the masses. Scholars have defined advertising as the process by which a product or service is introduced with the purpose of persuading the people of a locality to utilize that product or service. Others have also defined advertising as the process of introducing to the public an idea, product or Service through a paid announcement from a non-individual and identifiable source to encourage the public to make use of what is introduced.

Root (1994) defines advertising as any paid form of non-personal communication by an identified sponsor to promote a product or company. Advertising has been the dominant instrument of mass promotion of goods and services through planned advertising services. Advertising has been defined as the dissemination of information concerning an idea, service or product to compel action in accordance with the intent of the advertiser. The American Marketing Association defined advertising as 'any paid form of non-personal presentation of idea, goods or service by an identified sponsor.

This definition provides about 5 important elements of advertising which include—(a) advertising is a paid form of communication, (b) advertising is non-personal communication directed at specific target group, (c) advertising precisely promotes favourable ideas regarding the goods and services, (d) advertising is directed at the target group in order to create interest in them about the goods and services, and (e) advertising is issued by an identified sponsor who is interested in generating income through the sale of goods and services.

Shah and D'Souza (2009) identify the objectives of advertising which include—information, persuasion, reminder and reinforcement. The advertising messages generally inform the consumers about the salient features including the availability of goods and services. In the age of competitive business, advertising messages also persuade the customers to consume the goods and services by way of establishing superiority over other goods and services. The advertising messages remind the customers about the ways and means of fulfilling their requirements after purchasing the goods and services. The advertising services also seek to convince current customers that they have made the right choice by reinforcing key benefits and depicting satisfied customers of the brand. Advertising services are made available all over the world since they bestow a sort of authenticity to the goods and services.

Murthy and Bojanna (2010) define: "Advertising is a major way of establishing communication between the manufacturer and the consumer. Advertising acts as a reminder to the existing consumers and attracts new customers as well". Advertising is beneficial to both the parties, namely—advertisers and customers. The advertisers are able to establish direct rapport with the customers and build suitable brand image which enhances the salability of the goods and services. The customers are also given the benefit of education regarding the salient features of the goods and services including the price and availability of the goods and services. Advertising also facilitates economic growth by developing new market segments in the society.

Shah and D'Souza (2009) observe: "Advertising serves the primary purpose of generating awareness about the goods and services among the target group. Advertising and promotion form the crucial communication system for businesses and consumers. By communicating product information to the target audience, the advertising plays a key role in the marketing programmes of the advertisers. The consumers are also enabled by the advertising services to find out the goods and services of their choice. The increasing growth in advertising and media expenditure provides evidence of their rising significance in the modern society."

Advertising provides socially and economically beneficial services to the mankind. Modern business organizations gain immensely through advertising services. The consumers also get necessary information about the availability of goods and services which suit their convenience. Today, the goal of business promotion cannot be actualized in the absence of planned advertising services. Advertising services also dramatize the goods and services and trigger the sales of goods and services in a competitive environment.

The most common types of advertising are classified by the scholars on the basis of the nature or purpose of the advertisement. Prominent among them include—brand-building advertising, tactical advertising, national advertising, retail advertising, public service advertising, corporate advertising, primary-demand advertising, and business to business advertising.

The brand-building advertising usually focuses on creating product awareness and building brand image. The tactical advertising is usually aimed at marketing problem which can be solved through effective communication. The retail advertising is released by the retailers who sell the goods and services at grassroots level. The public service advertising is issued for non-profit reasons by the welfare organizations for the purpose of creating public awareness. The corporate advertising is meant for brand building which is issued by the corporate houses with a focus on production, price, utility and so on. The primary-demand advertising usually intends to build favourable demand for the goods and services. The selective-demand advertising aims at building demand for specific brand. The business to business advertising is directed at institutional customers rather than individual customers. The trade advertising is targeted to channel members like dealers, distributors and retailers. No organization can reach out to the customers and general publics in the absence of systematic advertising in the present times.

In this age of buyer-oriented economy, advertising has become an important means of promotion of goods and services. The customers are spread across the length and breadth of the world in the age of globalization of economy. Advertising campaigns are required to reach out to the various consumers since it primarily serves a marketing function by helping modern organizations which provide goods and services to the mankind advertising is always directed at a target audience which is a specific segment of the population for whom the goods and services have a definite appeal. A new branch of consumer advertising has emerged which is targeted at the people who buy goods and services for personal use. Hence, the advertisers are required to select and use media which are accessible, credible, persuasive and useful from the point of view of persuasive communication. The three main components of the advertising industry include—the advertisers, advertising agency and the media.

Advertising media consists of any means by which sales can be conveyed to potential buyers. The choice of media is immense in the developed countries but somewhat limited in the developing countries. As an advertising medium, anything can and has been used like tickets, matchbox, street utter bins, taxicabs, parking meters, shopping advertising media should have the sense of selection. Those who exploit anything to do with advertising media should have the sense of selection. Often it is seen that more money is spent to get less benefit, so skilful advertiser should always choose the right medium. That is why media buying is a skilled business the objective being to get the most effective advertising at the lowest cost.

In reality, the communications media serve as the bridge between the sellers and buyers of goods and services. The advertisers are required to utilize the services of skilled, specialized and competent media planners who can help them to place and schedule their advertisements. The advertisers are required to understand the reach, frequency, selectivity, efficiency and credibility of the traditional and modern media of advertising. The advertising agencies also help the advertisers to select the available best media of advertising. Broadly speaking, the media of advertising can be chosen on the basis of first hand information, personal observation, authentic data and experts' suggestions under the normal circumstances. The media of advertising include—print media, electronic media, outdoor media and new media.

The print media are the oldest means of mass media which primarily include newspapers and magazines. The print media provide detailed advertising services to the consumers. The newspapers have a wider reach and they can go to any geographic location and attract the attention of the consumers. The magazines are known for limited reach when compared to newspapers. But, the magazines offer a tremendous degree of selectivity for advertisers. The electronic media of communication, namely radio and television provide competitive advertising services across the globe. In the present times, television has become the most prominent medium of advertising as compared to the radio.

The print media enjoy the long life span and receive more advertising revenue. Modern advertising executives are aware that online classified-advertising services are taking a bite out of industry revenues. The newspapers are facing challenge from online advertising in the present times. Analysts have pointed out that advertising through print media brings a definite competitive advantage despite the growth of Internet.

The outdoor advertising services reach out to the people at the grassroots level through attractive and creative advertising services. The outdoor media are the oldest established form of advertising which include—posters, banners, transit media (combination of transit and billboard), displays in bus station, railway station and airport, kiosks and showcases, interior displays, mobile displays, hoarding, attention grabbers, wall writings. These outdoor media reach out to the people in rural and urban areas since they are economically viable and culturally friendly means of advertising.

The Internet has become the ultimate direct marketing medium and fastest growing advertising medium in the world. Besides Internet, there are other interactive new media of advertising which facilitate active participation from interactivity point of view with the users. Prominent among them include—mobile telephony, computer games, kiosk-based terminals, interactive television, electronic storage media and so on. In this age of integrated marketing communication, traditional and modern media of advertising are widely utilized by the community of advertisers.

The process of Industrial Revolution paved the way for institutionalization of business all over the world. In the beginning, few manufacturing agencies provided limited goods and services. There was a kind of seller-oriented economy which did not demand any kind of persuasive communication in the name of advertising. Subsequently business houses were established everywhere in order to reach out to various publics including the customers who became the controllers of economy. In the beginning there were outdoor advertising and print advertisements which were known for limited coverage and impact. As the economy expanded during the 19th century, business promotion activities including advertising management grew alongside. Advertising also became a specialized branch of business management. Advertising executives were trained in the schools of business management and mass communication and journalism in India and elsewhere.

The growth of electronic media including television paved the way for electronic advertising. The introduction of cable television and particularly MTV ushered in a new era of advertising. Marketing through the Internet and other new media opened new frontiers for advertisers and contributed to the 'dotcom boom' of the 1990s. Commercial advertising and public service advertising were developed in order to promote commercial goods and services and motivate the people about non-commercial issues such as human rights, environmental protection, gender justice, social justice, political ideology, progressive movements and so on.

Advertising is an instrument of economic growth since it facilitates better marketing, consumption and profit oriented opportunities. Advertising has become increasingly prevalent in modern society. It occupies public space considerably, observes George Franck (1998). The communications media have also earned sizable chunk of their revenue through advertisements. The critics of advertising have called it as a necessary evil since it is a new kind of dictatorship which cannot be avoided, states Hanno Rauterberg (2008).

Advertising has become one of the major pillars of capitalist economy. McChesney (2008) has noted that advertising is part of the bone marrow of corporate capitalism which cannot function and establish global production and distribution networks in its absence. Manfred Knoche (2005) has even gone one step ahead by calling advertising not only a necessary evil but necessary elixir of life for the media business, the economy and capitalism of the whole.

Advertising has also become the producer's weapon in the competition for customer relationship management and trade advertising.

Kalle Lasn (1999) has termed advertising as the most prevalent and toxic of the mental pollutants in the age of globalization. Advertising services manufacture new desires and dreams in the minds of the people including women, youth and children according to empirical evidence. The commercial advertisements broadcast in radio and televisions are also known for greatest access and popularity regardless of time and space. The young generation is also addicted to advertisements which create a dream world based on glorification and reinforcement of certain values and beliefs.

Lasch (2001) argues that advertising leads to an overall increase in the consumption in modern society. Advertising not only popularizes the goods and services but promotes consumption as a way of life in reality. The courts have also seriously taken note of the ill effects of advertising on the mankind as a matter of judicial activism. Several legal restrictions are placed upon the advertising campaigns in Asia, Latin America, Middle East, Europe, America and elsewhere. Several activists have called upon the governments to ensure constant vigilance over the advertisements which mar the health and progress of the mankind as a matter of social responsibility.

George Frank (1998) has criticized the role of advertising which is part of 'mental capitalism' led by the champions of globalization. Advertising has become a billion-dollar business in the world in the new millennium. The industry is accused of being one of the engines powering a convoluted economic mass production system which promotes consumption, observes Sut Jhully (2009). The critic has cautioned that contemporary advertising would destroy the world culturally and otherwise if necessary checks and balances are not ensured by the right thinking in the visuals and organizations. Scholars have also examined the relationship between the price of attention and hidden costs in relation to modern advertising campaigns launched by the capitalist forces.

Advertising has become an important instrument of manufacturing the consent of the people more or less making use of associations, emotions and drives dormant in the sub-conscience of people. McChesney (2008) states: "All human needs, relationships and fears—the deepest recessed of the human psyche—become mere means for the expansion of the commodity universe under the force of modern marketing. With the rise to prominence of modern marketing, commercialism—the translation of human relations into commodity relations—although a phenomenon intrinsic to capitalism, has expanded exponentially.

Lasch (1995) argues that advertising takes on the role of a life councillor in matters of attraction since it manufactures a culture of Narcissism. Advertising is practiced by the capitalists on the basis of certain psychological theories about how to create subjects, enabling advertising and marketing to take on a more clearly psychological tinge according to Miller and Rose (2009). The advertisers have realized that the same things can be endowed with different intended meanings for different individuals and groups of people, thereby offering mass produced visions of individualism. Advertising research has focused the attention of the world on the other side of advertising even though the efficiency of the advertising has improved over a period of time. The advertising and marketing firms are heavily criticized by the researchers and critics for the advertising onslaught against the mankind. This development has been termed as an ongoing threat to democratic culture by Giroux (2009).

In the age of globalization, the media have become a branch of the contemporary advertising industry since they are primarily dependent on the advertisers. This dependency has distinct implications for the nature of media content, according to McChesney (2008). The media professionals too have accepted the economics of advertising which produces media contents for the benefit of advertisers and capitalists. The media institutions are forced to remain at the receiving end and create conducive advertising environment in order to secure constant advertising revenue by sacrificing their corporate social responsibility. The borders between advertising and media have become more blurred. The commercial basis of media and advertising has caused a death blow to the human values and democratic institutions.

James Rorty (1976) comments: "The Gargoyle's mouth is a loudspeaker, powered by the vested interest of a two-billion dollar industry, and backs of that the vested interests of business as a whole, of industry, of finance. It is never silent, it drowns out all other voices and it suffers no rebuke, for it is not the voice of America. The contents of modern advertising truly represent the voice of their master rather than the people including the consumers who have become silent victims of advertising which is the component of capitalism. The advertising is shaping the values of modern society wherein the stimuli of art, science and religion are progressively expelled to the periphery of American life."

Advertising has also brought about a new era of commercialization of culture since it is integrated into modern life style and fashion. The sports sector is also grossly affected by the advertising industry since it has brought about new environment which is devoid of healthy sports culture. In sports the media are able to generate enormous sales in both circulation and advertising, writes McChesney (2008). Sports sponsorship is undertaken by the leading industrial houses which have polluted the environment and destroyed the sportsmanship across the globe. Advertising has become an all pervasive activity which has brought about commercialization of culture, public space and other vital sectors of development.

Sut Jhully (2006) has rightly considered advertising as a kind of religion which has replaced the human values and aspirations in the contemporary economy led by the market forces. Corporate advertising has reduced the young generation to consumers. Critics have noted that corporate advertising has hijacked the human values, progressive movements and democratic culture all over the world. It is also accused of reinforcing stereo types and deliberately promoting sexism, racism, ageism and other factors which have impeded the progress of mankind. The regulations which have prohibited negative advertisements have been neglected by the advertising industry. The campaigns against malicious and negative advertisements have been neglected by the state which is controlled by the money power, muscle power, media power and so on. Progressive mass movements have critically opposed the prevailing sorry state of affairs which have cropped up because of the negative influence of advertising. New regulations are not strictly implemented by the government bodies and law enforcement agencies in the absence of powerful public activism.

The concept of corporate advertising is somewhat different from that of product advertising. There are several additional factors that should be taken into consideration while understanding the true nature of corporate advertising in modern society. It is a specialized advertising service which primarily lays emphasis on corporate identity which has a bearing on the salability of the goods and services manufactured by modern corporate houses. Basically, corporate advertising comprises not merely the end users but the internal employees as well as the business associates. Modern corporate houses are required to choose the best promotional tools, technologies and techniques which come under the purview of corporate advertising. Usually, the corporate communication department of an organization handles the corporate advertising activities which are meant for promoting the image of the organization.

The corporate advertising is done over the mass media to promote the company's image according to Shah and D'Souza (2009). The corporate advertising managers are primarily responsible for the enhancement of brand knowledge and maximization of the brand performance within a marketing environment which is practically beyond their control. The corporate advertising is a substantial business activity, with expenditures now exceeding $9 billion according to Belch and Belch (1996).

In reality, corporate advertising is a challenging task which is responsible for influencing the behaviours of the consumers in favour of the corporate house, goods and services especially in a competitive business environment. Scholars lilke Cowles, Garbett and Rothschild have examined the role of corporate advertising in the enhancement of corporate image. Other studies have also primarily dealt with the investment made by the corporate houses on corporate advertising management. Prominent among them include—Haley, Javalgi *et al.*, Schumann, Hathcote and West. Corporate advertising is also primarily responsible for the creation of constructive, positive and meaningful brands according to Javalgi *et al.*, Winkleman and Winters.

Corporate advertising is consciously practiced by the corporate houses in order to promote favourable consumers' brand knowledge according to Keller, Loken and Roedder John, MacInnis, Moorman, and Jaworski and Rao and Sieben. These studies have revealed that consumer's beliefs about and attitudes towards brand ads can directly influence their brand knowledge. Homer, MacKenzie, Lutz, and Belch have explored the role of corporate advertising which is designed to market a specific brand in order to affect consumers' brand knowledge.

In reality, corporate advertising is managed with a view to control the messages, execution, and placement of brand advertising. However, they cannot control its effects, which depend on factors such as clutter, consumers' involvement level, and competitive actions under the normal circumstances. Despite certain limitations, brand managers can use certain tactics that may encourage consumers to use their corporate advertising knowledge when processing brand information. Practically, the brand managers may influence consumers' use of it in a brand information processing context according to the empirical evidence.

The corporate advertising managers are also required to treat the corporate advertising environment as an exogenous factor on the basis of certain models which are related to conceptualization and practical implementation of corporate advertising. These models also enable the advertising managers to integrate relevant research concepts taken from the marketing, psychology, and consumer behaviour literatures and derive several testable propositions which practically benefit the corporate houses. Experts have suggested certain norms and guidelines which enhance the success of corporate advertising. They have suggested that advertising elements need not be incorporated in the campaigns and product packaging. Experience reveals that advertising elements must stand alone and may not be combined with any other object such as logos, words, graphics, photos, slogans, numbers, design features, or symbols.

Advertising has become a new way of life especially in the age of globalization. Modern corporations have to reach out to the people through various advertising campaigns in order to enhance the salability of the goods and services manufactured by them. Advertising has also become a prominent instrument of corporate reputation management over a period of time. Commercial advertisers primarily seek to generate increased consumption of their goods and services through systematic branding which involves the repetition of an image or product name in an effort to associate related qualities with the brand in the minds of consumers. Traditional and modern communications media are used to deliver the messages in order to invite the attention of the consumers and persuade them to accept the goods and services manufactured by various public and private corporations. The money spent on corporate advertising has increased considerably over a period of time.

Good corporate advertising acts as an umbrella covering all the products and services associated with a company. Any corporate advertising campaign should be both strategic, looking towards the future of the company and aligned with its mission, and consistent, aligning with the products and services that the company sells. An effective corporate advertising campaign also needs to be part of an overall communication strategy designed to establish and build corporate reputation, presenting the company's identity in a way that reinforces other company-initiated messages.

Corporate reputation building is indeed a challenging task. According to Haapaniemi and Schwartz, it takes a long time to build a reputation, but it can be destroyed overnight in a single event. Devine states that reputation acts as a gauge, defining and giving an organization its sense of identity. Hanson and Stuart and Barney concur that corporate reputations once created are relatively steadfast. Of all bases of differentiation, none is more difficult to duplicate than an organization's reputation.

Scholars have identified four business parameters that influence corporate reputation, namely—general business management, financial management, corporate marketing and corporate communication. These parameters are widely discussed since they primarily include leadership and management qualities, organizational ethics, shareholder value, organizational sustainability, corporate branding, the marketing mix, public relations and relationships with stakeholders. This is in line with Schreiber who considers that these variables are similar to those used in the yearly *Fortune* magazine rankings of 'America's Most Admired Corporations'.

Klein reports that financial executives believe that a CEO's reputation would influence them to buy shares in the organization. Nakra maintains that successful global leaders earn a reputation for credibility among investors by showing profitability to individual and institutional shareholders, maintaining a stable return on investment and nurturing financial growth prospects. Ettorre suggests that intelligent organizations make perception management part of their senior executive training regime, enabling a greater understanding of corporate branding and resultant corporate reputation. Schreiber argues that executives often misunderstand how reputations are achieved and maintained. As a result, they rely too heavily on corporate advertising, while at the same time not doing enough about reputation-building activities with stakeholders.

Hall and Barban (1987) have pointed out that corporate houses are required to sustain the institutional reputation since it is the foundation upon which the prosperity of corporate houses is cherished. He has also noted that delivery of people-friendly goods and services and sustenance of public good would constantly safeguard the reputation of corporate houses. O'Connor and Wilson concur that a key reason to set metrics for reputation management is to meet today's demand for transparency and governance structures. In this context, reputation, of which the public relations practitioner is custodian, is now an organization's most valuable and fragile asset.

The corporate houses are also required to identify and incorporate certain healthy elements of financial managements since it is vital for the progress of organizations. Klein asserts that the motivation to rush to reputation management and measurement is evidence that a good reputation can dramatically affect an organization's results. Psychologically, an organization with a solid reputation earns the benefit of the doubt in times of crisis. Good public relations professionals know that a lot is at stake in their work of protecting and enhancing corporate reputation, especially in terms of building and maintaining relationships with stakeholders. Financial management elements are acknowledged to form a major portion of the aspects that influence investment decisions and corporate reputation.

Gary, Smeltzer and McNaughton have stated that a favourable reputation is regarded as a prerequisite to success in the global financial marketplace. Shareholders can ultimately give or withhold their approval of management through their votes based on their perception of an organization's corporate reputation. Studies have also primarily dealt with the fundamental relationship between corporate advertising and globalization. Van der Walt *et al.* have highlighted the fact that modern corporate houses must have competitive advantages over competitors. In today's interlinked world as described by Mastal, corporate reputation, which is the cumulative perceptions of an organization by its key stakeholders, is increasingly recognized for its bottom-line impact.

In reality, empirical studies have revealed that corporate houses with good reputations achieve higher-than-average profitability compared with their peer groups. Grupp and Gaines-Ross have also pointed out that corporate reputation matters most in the present competitive business environment not only from income generating point of view but also from the sustainable development of corporate houses point of view. Experience has also revealed that in the age of globalization, advertising has become a prominent instrument of profit making.

Richardson and Bolesh have noted that reputable organizations protect their corporate images by maintaining high standards of practice no matter what the circumstances. The most admired organizations use commitment to quality products and services to build and maintain their reputations. Van der Walt *et al.* have noted that the price is the only element which produces income to the corporate house since it has the most immediate and direct impact on an organization's profitability, which has an influence on corporate reputation. Alsop has rightly argued that product quality, innovation and good value are crucial factors which are associated with the corporate reputation of public and private undertakings.

Marketing communication has become an important tool of projecting the positive and beneficial effects of the goods and services offered by the corporate houses. Van der Walt *et al.*, Dowling, Christensen and Askegaard have interpreted the marketing communications as an attempt made by the corporate houses to project their 'ideal self-image' to both internal and external stakeholders, which will have an impact on corporate reputation. Nakra notes that corporate reputation emanates from all the business activities and communications it undertakes intentionally and unintentionally in the marketplace, such as advertising, promotion, direct marketing, personal selling, trade relations, public relations and community relations. Different stakeholders view a corporation differently because they focus on and look at different parts of the organization.

Saxton argues that all stakeholders of corporate houses are usually affected by the brand image and ultimately the corporate reputation created through advertising and other marketing communication activities. Miller suggests that one way to help reputation is to deal effectively with the media in regard to corporate advertising management. The organization needs to respond while the news is breaking and not after there has been time to decide what is to be said. Mastal notes that an organization's message strategy should reflect its corporate position as well as the position it is taking on the issues. Organizations that have strong reputations generally have three or four key messages they recite over and over in all media and to all key stakeholders.

Corporate advertising has considerable impact on the corporate reputation of modern organizations regardless of space and time. Grupp and Gaines-Ross emphasise that corporate communicators should handle the advertising operations which would contribute decisively towards enhancing corporate reputation and driving market value for the goods and services. The corporate leaders and communicators are also required to monitor and evaluate the impact of corporate advertising and find out how communication of corporate and product messages are linked to a change in perceptions and behaviour among their key stakeholders, as well as to financial and shareholder returns. By identifying corporate advertising objectives, tools, techniques and operations should be evaluated through proper qualitative and quantitative research methods. Zyglidopoulos and Phillips suggest that every corporate house must be aware of the different concerns of various stakeholders when choosing a reputation-building strategy *vis-à-vis* corporate advertising.

The clients of various corporate houses also play a crucial role in the process of corporate reputation building according to Johnson and Richardson and Bolesh. The scholars have noted that corporate houses should build good reputation which attracts the attention of various clients and other stakeholders through series of effective corporate communication and advertising campaigns. They have further highlighted the need for two-way communication which builds client confidence. Miller, Richardson and Bolesh have clearly emphasized that there is no magic formula for corporate reputation which enables the corporate houses to maintain and reinforce their credibility, popularity, status and prospects. Scholars have rightly observed that corporate advertising campaigns should be guided by certain healthy parameters and practices in order to safeguard public interest in the age of globalization.

Economic analysts have predicted that the advertising revenue would double to $30 million and grow at the rate of 32 per cent per year. Corporate advertising has become the most important tool in the marketing of products and services in the changed economic environment. Companies universally accepted this fact. The expenses on advertising are considered to be a profitable investment that reaps profits both in the long and short run. Businesses that keep on advertising regardless of rise or fall in the economic times get a competitive advantage over those that cut their advertisement budgets.

The main technological difference between traditional media advertising and online display advertising is that online, advertisements are served to targeted individual customers in real time, whereas in traditional media, targeting is done through broader categories such as demographic and socio-economic groups. Although the cost of advertising is quite high but the benefits in the long run balance the high cost involved in the practice of advertising. The television attracts maximum advertising revenue when compared to other mass media. The online advertising has also grown rapidly in the new millennium. It now accounts for almost one-seventh of all advertising budget and contributes to the preponderance of revenues for most websites. It is projected to increase sharply as more consumers spend time online on their personal computers and as additional devices such as mobile phones and televisions are connected to the web. The online advertising industry has revolutionized many aspects of an age-old business and the unique features of online advertising include the use of Internet-based technologies and data collection mechanisms. These devices target and track specific individuals since they are based on tested economic and statistical methods.

Internet-based technologies are revolutionizing the stodgy $750 billion global advertising industry, according to the latest statistics. The Internet has changed the contemporary advertising scenario by allowing advertisers to target specific individuals and paying only when those individuals click on the advertisements. More sophisticated technologies are beginning to track not only whether individuals clicked on an advertisement but whether that actually translated into a sale. Search-based advertising has been developed as the most advanced methods for targeting consumers and charging for results. These new technologies are critically important for understanding the significance of corporate advertising in the age of globalization.

Impact of Globalization on Corporate Communication in the World

An era of globalization of economy began in the last quarter of the 20th century. Globalization of economy also became a full-fledged activity in the 1990s. Rapid expansion of economy in general and public and private undertakings in particular took place with the entry of Multi-National Corporations. These undertakings evolved and introduced new concepts of management of which Corporate Communication is an important dimension. In the age of globalization, the corporate sector has been witnessing revolutionary changes in organizational and operational conditions. The overall corporate environment is more competitive and global than ever before.

The word 'corporate' refers to the business setting in which corporate communication emerged as a separate function along side human resources management, financial resources management, materials management, operations management and so on. The word 'communication' refers to the occurrence of continuous dialogue between the management and various stakeholders. Communication is indeed the life blood of modern corporate houses. Thus, 'corporate communication' becomes a cementing force, binding force and driving force in modern organizations. Broadly speaking, corporate communication can be identified as the management function that is responsible for coordinating the work done by organizational communicators in different specialized disciplines such as employee relations, investor relations, supplier relations, distributor relations, consumer relations, media relations, government relations, community relations and so on.

The field of corporate management is being enriched by addition of new concepts and practices to the management vocabulary on a regular basis. In this new economic environment, one of the stupendous tasks of corporate management is to bridge the communication gap between the management and employees on the one hand and between the organization and constituent publics on the other hand. Corporate Communication has emerged as a prominent management function of our times. The essentiality of this function is seldom questioned in the present age of competitiveness. The development of communications media has widened the horizon of

Corporate Communication which encompasses a large number of stakeholders both inside and outside the organization. Corporate Communication is rightly perceived as an instrument of organizational development in all modern organizations. Many scholars have studied the role of Corporate Communication in different contexts all over the world.

In a world that constantly grows complex, sophisticated and even bigger, the need for two-way persuasive Corporate Communication becomes inevitable in the modern society. In a democratic society, the constituent publics have a right to information, right to participation, right to agitation and right to empowerment. Hence, Corporate Communication provides opportunities for meaningful dialogue between modern organizations and various stakeholders. The harmonious functioning of government and corporate houses demands organized Corporate Communication. Corporate Communication serves a variety of organizations in modern times. It is an approach to problems by itself. Any modern organization that deals with various publics has a need for Corporate Communication.

Today, political parties, religious institutions, cultural organizations, voluntary organizations, educational institutions, business organizations, industrial organizations, trade unions, government organizations, NGOs—all need systematic and sustainable Public Relations activities which are now broadly practiced as Corporate Communication. The tools of Corporate Communication include—publicity, propaganda, lobbying, advertising, persuasion, etc. Corporate Communication plays an important role in modern organizations. It is necessary to understand the stakeholders in modern society. Prominent among them include—employees, shareholders, suppliers, distributors, consumers, media professionals, government servants, local citizens and so on. It enables modern organizations and constituent publics to maintain mutually beneficial relationships.

Fombrun and Van Riel (2004) define Corporate Communication as 'an instrument of management by means of which all consciously used forms of internal and external communication are harmonized as effectively and efficiently as possible', with the overall objective of creating 'a favourable basis for relationships with groups upon which the company is dependent'.

Corporate Communication obviously involves a whole range of managerial activities which become complete and meaningful with the application of appropriate technologies and strategies. Broadly speaking, Corporate Communication is a management function that offers a framework for the effective coordination of all internal and external communication with the overall purpose of establishing and maintaining favourable reputations with stakeholder groups upon which the organization is dependent. The Corporate Communication becomes complex in large organizations which have a wide geographical range, such as multinational corporations, or with a wide range of products or services, where the coordination of communication is often a balancing act between corporate headquarters and the various divisions and business units involved.

Marchand (1998) observed that Corporate Communication had emerged as the prominent instrument of organizational management over a period of time. Corporate Communication is an art and science of developing a reciprocal understanding, goodwill, cooperation and support between modern organizations and stakeholders. It facilitates image building, institution building, nation building, problem solving, crisis management and other challenging tasks of modern times. Corporate Communicators are required to gain absolute knowledge, experience, expertise and competence in order to cope with various needs, challenges and demands. Hence, modern organizations require specialists in various aspects Corporate Communication management in the age of competitiveness.

The emerging trends and developments in the global economic environment and the corresponding transition in the management and communication policies in the world have made the managements realize the importance of Corporate Communication. Scott M. Cutlip, Allen H. Center and Glen M. Broom (2004) have emphasized the need and importance of Corporate Communication thus: "Organizational adjustment is the outcome of Public Relations which suggests at management level, policy influencing role and calls for corrective action in addition to communication." Corporate Communication is not merely confined to that of presenting the points of view of the organization but to prevail upon the leaders of the organization to reconcile or adjust in the public interest those aspects of corporate behaviour which have a social significance in modern society.

Otis Baskin, Craig Aronoff and Dan Lattimore (1977) emphasize the role of Corporate Communication in the age of globalization thus: "In a complex global society, business, government, non-profit and other organizations must have people who can communicate the needs of the organization to its various constituents and, at the same time, communicate the concerns of those publics back to the organization. In this environment of rapid social change, every organization must evolve or die. Corporate Communicators must possess the communications expertise and social sensitivity necessary to help organizations adapt themselves to changing environments."

Corporate Communication is required to establish, maintain and sustain mutually acceptable and rewarding relationships between the organization and its various publics. Without effective people-friendly, cause-oriented, mission-oriented and progress-oriented Corporate Communication it is not possible to achieve progress in this age of competitiveness. According to Dave Ulrich (1998), "Corporate Communication activities in modern organizations usually serve three important purposes. First, a host of communication tools and techniques may be used to hold managers implement initiatives. Second, communication with employees may focus less on particular initiatives and more on building employee bonds with the firm and with the managers of the firm. Third, communication may increase commitment from those outside the firm by way of shareholder updates, (e.g. annual reports, investor relations, meetings etc.), customer information, (e.g. product literature), and other public relation efforts (e.g. advertising a firm's identity)".

Corporate communication is a planned, organized and systematic management function that offers a sound framework for the effective coordination of all internal and external communication with the ultimate objective of establishing and maintaining mutually beneficial human relationship between the organization and various stakeholders in order to sustain reputation which matters most in the present age of competitive business. "Corporate Communication demands an integrated approach to manage the organizational communication and it transcends the specialties of individual communication practitioners. Corporate Communication is indeed a critical factor which is associated with corporate reputation management", notes Argenti (1996). Corporate communicators are required to develop suitable professional vision and assume the role of missionaries of organizational development.

Argenti (1998) conducted the most exhaustive study of Corporate Communication in the past half-century. He also studied the development of Corporate Communication system on the basis of a more strategic rather than reactive approach to organizational communication. He observes: "Corporate Communication practitioners agree that communicating effectively with employees is the most important area of Corporate Communication which will emerge as a separate management function with an important role in corporate management". The employees are indeed the backbone of organizational development. They must be motivated to work harder when the management communicates with them honestly and regularly.

Michael (1996) focuses the role of Corporate Communication thus: "Corporate Communication has been studied by different scholars as a peripheral part of human resource management and organizational behaviour. The growth of theories of communication has resulted in the realization of the importance of communication in corporate sector since it is an important means of counselling and guidance in modern organizations." Corporate Communication provides necessary basis for meaningful understanding and interactions between the management and employees. It is necessary in modern organizations to supervise the functions of the employees and motivate them for better participation and performance.

Keith Davis (1977) has made an elaborate survey of the working of communication functions in an organization and was the first scholar to recommend that communication systems should be handled by the specialists. He comments: "Communication is the life-blood of modern organizations. Without constant communication flow, organizations cannot establish good rapport with the employees and other constituent publics. In particular, the management should cultivate an everlasting relationship with various stakeholders who are the backbone of organizational development." The scholar focused on the role of managers in maintaining a healthy communication system in modern organizations.

Downs *et al.* (1977) examined the various aspects of communication pertaining to the organizational context. They also analyzed the organizational communication from the systems perspective and identified the contextual factors that assist or constrain the organizational communicator. They observe: "There is a need for a natural wedlock between communication theory and organizational theory. The modern managements should develop suitable organizational communication networks and put forth planned, sustainable and organized efforts to bridge the communication gap between the organization and constituent publics. The organizational communication activities should be managed by the specialists in communication." The scholars have analyzed the various aspects of organizational communication and called upon the modern managements to create corporate communication networks in order to achieve the goals of organization.

Following Fayol and Taylor's principles of scientific management, the emphasis shifted to maximizing productivity and competitiveness by optimizing the utilization of capital resources and human resources. Effective Human Resources Management (HRM) started with Elton Mayo's Human Relations thought which put a greater emphasis on organizational communication. A new discipline called Corporate Communication emerged on account of rapid strides in economy, management and information technology which necessitated greater research in this area. In this context, organizational management and Corporate Communication form an inevitable link among the corporate body and constituent publics.

Kotler, Mindak, Cutlip, Argenti and other scholars evaluated the nature, scope and significance of corporate communication in their writings. A new body of scholarship emerged on various aspects of corporate communication all over the world. Revolutionary changes in the field of communication science and technology have added a new dimension to the practice of Corporate Communication. Modern corporate houses consciously developed corporate communication departments and recruited trained corporate communicators in order to build and sustain corporate reputation. The Corporate Communication System, process and practices are subjected to scientific evaluation across the globe.

Corporate Communication has emerged over the years as a prominent two-way persuasive communication in modern organizations in a developing country like India. Corporate

Communication is a relatively new concept for which there is no consensus on a precise definition. However, experts have defined Corporate Communication on the basis of specific tools, media, techniques and operations listed under the comprehensive banner of Corporate Communication. Corporate Communication is the process that translates corporate identity into corporate image since it plays a pivotal role in safeguarding the image and interests of modern organizations. It also provides the means for the modern organizations to adjust themselves to the changing corporate environment in general. It also facilitates meaningful and mutually beneficial understanding and transactions between the organization and various stakeholders in the modern society. The role of Corporate Communication is crucial in the entire process because without effective communication the values, strategies and activities of the organization will never be understood by the various stakeholders in the age of globalization.

Summary

The relationship between communication and globalization is widely discussed in the new millennium. Media institutions have grown in the world as profit oriented industries in the age of globalization. The growth of communication from stone writing to the level of Internet is a marvelous journey and fascinating story. After Gutenberg's invention of the movable printing press in 1468 and the emergence of newspapers thereafter, the world witnessed early mass media services. The world also witnessed several milestones in the growth and development of communication media such as black and white photograph by Fox Talbot (1939), electric telegraphy (1853), the first movie by the Lumiere Brothers (1895), the invention of the phonograph by Edison (1896), the wireless radio by Marconi (1912), and the first television transmission (1936). In the last quarter of the 20th century, new media of communication like telecommunication, satellite communication and online communication emerged as effective means of interactive communication. The new millennium has witnessed another set of advanced media tools and technologies known as social media which have emerged as alternative media for the people. In the present times, the media have become service and profit oriented institutions. The media institutions have been greatly influenced by the process of globalization and switched over to profit-centred communication channels. The ethical, legal and social aspects of media management are examined by the scholars across the globe in order to ensure effective checks and balances which would make various communications media accountable to the people in the age of globalization.

4

Globalization and Indian Media

Introduction

India has emerged as a major media power in the world. The Indian media was initiated since the late 18th century with print media in 1780, radio broadcasting initiated in 1927, the screening of Auguste and Louis Lumière moving pictures in Bombay initiated in 1895, the telecasting of Doordarshan programmes in 1959, the launching of new media in 1990s and functioning of social media in the new millennium. The Constitution of India guarantees the freedom of speech and expression to all the citizens including the media professionals. The constitutional provisions clearly indicate the media freedom, responsibility and accountability in Indian context. The country produced 100 million newspaper copies, contained more than 800 radio stations, 1,400 television stations and 1,000 feature films per year as of 2012. In this section, impact of globalization on Indian economy and media, impact of Foreign Direct Investment (FDI) on Indian media (print, electronic, film, NCTs, folk media), corporate advertising and corporate communication are examined.

Impact of Globalization on Indian Economy

India had achieved commendable economic progress under the leadership of Buddha 2500 years ago. Ashoka played a historical role in making India an economic super power. The rulers who succeeded Ashoka sustained the developmental legacy of India effectively. The Buddhist rulers followed the economic philosophy of Buddha and created an egalitarian society in India long before the occurrence of industrial revolution in the West. India became economically and politically weak under the rule of Hindu fundamentalists led by Manu who refused equality to women and weaker sections for reasons best known to him. The caste system was created by the fundamentalists in order to maintain status-quoism which weakened the Indian society. The practice of untouchability was also responsible for the exclusion of the indigenous people of India from the mainstream of development. This tendency paved the way for about 1000 years of foreign rule and poor economic status of the people of India.

Several national leaders in India like Phuley, Kabir, Ambedkar, Periyar, Narayan Guru and others strongly advocated that social and economic equality should be established in India on the basis of human values. India earned the national freedom in 1947 under the dedicated leadership of Mahatma Gandhi who advocated the welfare of all Indians economically and otherwise. He gave a '*Sarvodaya*' model of development which stood by the development of all Indians. His contemporary Ambedkar fought against social and economic inequity and gave another '*Antyodaya*' model of development which stood by the development of the last man of the Indian society. Ambedkar strongly advocated that the goal of Sarvodaya should be achieved through Antyodaya since he was committed to the welfare and progress of all Indians.

In the post-Independence era, the national leaders adopted the Constitution of India which was drafted by Ambedkar and other legal luminaries. The Indian Constitution contains series of progressive measures for the empowerment of the people of India regardless of religion, region, gender, caste, creed and so on. Unfortunately, the rulers adopted Western model of development which did not suit the Indian environment. The Constitutional provisions were not strictly implemented by the rulers in the post-Independence era in India. The women and weaker sections of the Indian society were excluded, isolated and annihilated from the points of view of social justice and economic development.

India opened up the economy in the early nineties following a major crisis caused led by a foreign exchange crunch that dragged the economy close to defaulting on loans. The process of liberalization of Indian economy in the name of economic globalization was launched by the then Prime Minister P.V. Narasimha Rao and Manmohan Singh who was Finance Minister in 1991. The new economic reform, popularly known as, liberalization, privatization and globalization (LPG model) aimed at making the Indian economy as fastest growing economy and globally competitive. The major measures were initiated as a part of the liberalization and globalization strategy in the early nineties included the following:

- Devaluation.
- Disinvestment.
- Dismantling of the industrial licensing regime.
- Allowing Foreign Direct Investment.
- Non-Resident Indian scheme throwing open industries reserved for the public sector to private participation.
- Abolition of the (MRTP) Act.
- The removal of quantitative restrictions on imports.
- The reduction of the peak customs tariff.
- Wide-ranging financial sector reforms.

Series of reforms undertaken in the economic sector paved the way for remarkable increase in the GDP and growth rate of the national economy. In the age of globalization, India's economic growth has been high, exports have boomed, incidence of poverty has been reduced, employment has surged, begging by India for economic aid has stopped, long-term inflation rate has gone down, scarcity of goods have disappeared, the quality of products available have improved substantially and overall India has become progressively vibrant and internationally competitive according to the defenders of economic liberalization. The economists have stated that the service sector is the lifeline for the social economic growth of a country. There is considerable growth of the service sector like banking, insurance, trade, commerce, entertainment, etc. The rate of growth of the Gross Domestic Product (GDP) of India increased from 5.6 per cent during 1980-90 to 7 per cent in the 1993-2012 period. India has also achieved progress in respect of market capitalization. India has become one of the top five exporters of services amongst developing countries. In reality, satisfactory growth of imports was registered in financial services and communication services despite the global financial crisis. The defenders of globalization have also observed that India is in a stronger position to gain from international trade and investment. India has risen to the top of the IT industry in the world which is a reflection of the abundance of skilled manpower in the country. The economists have also cut an optimistic note about the increasing skilled manpower in the IT sector in India. The Foreign Direct Investment (FDI) has brought about in the rapid economic growth of most of the Southeast Asian countries including China and India.

The country can also attract greater foreign investment on the basis of acceleration of national economic growth with stability. The agriculture sector has not witnessed any progress in the age of globalization which has lowered the per capita income of the farmers and increased the rural indebtedness. The agricultural growth of 3.2 per cent observed from 1980 to 1997 decelerated to two per cent subsequently. The low agricultural growth has serious implications for the inclusive of growth of national economy since about 65 per cent of the people in the country primarily depend on agriculture for their survival and progress. The farmers are committing suicide since they are sidelined by the policy makers. The workers have not gained the benefit of gainful employment opportunities. The youth have not received professional skill development, employment generation, economic empowerment and allied benefits. The women have not achieved progress since they are excluded from the mainstream of development.

Amartya Sen observed that the rich became richer and the poor became poorer after the introduction of economic globalization in India and other developing nations. In the age of globalization, the capitalists, leaders, bureaucrats, traders and middlemen flourished. The farmers, workers, weaker sections and women became the victims of circumstances. Thus, India experienced the bright side and dark sides of globalization economically over a period of time. In the present times, India is experiencing series of political and economic omissions and commissions which have cost the national economy dearly. China achieved commendable progress in the age of globalization but India faced series of disadvantages due to several factors. India is also facing the problem of political corruption which is the main cause for economic crisis. Economists have critically analyzed the impact of globalization on Indian economy. India is facing several challenges of globalization in the present times. Prominent among them include—achieving the growth rate of 9-10 per cent, expansion of industry, promotion of agricultural sector, rejuvenation of cottage industry, development of urban and rural infrastructure, achievement of fiscal consolidation, employment generation, protection of domestic culture, empowering the people and so on. In India, there is increasing rural-to-urban shift of population. The market economy seems to be more concerned with the growth of consumerism to attract the high income groups who are urban-centred.

India is yet to achieve progress in order to wrest maximum benefits out of international trade and investment. The champions of globalization have insisted that the national leaders should delink the environmental standards and labour related considerations from trade negotiations. The developed nations are using India and other developing nations as dumping yard. There is only free rather than fair trade in India. The developed countries are known for double speak which has resulted in the heavy lobbying in India to protect labour. The economic concerns of India are not addressed properly. The domestic support to agriculture by developed countries constitutes a major stumbling block to third world trade expansion.

A greater integration of the Indian economy with the rest of the world is unavoidable. The Indian leaders and people are required to learn to swim in the tempestuous waters of competition in the age of globalization. India must prepare itself to meet the new challenges so that it will not be bypassed by this huge wave of technological and institutional changes. India has to achieve the goal of economic self-reliance through infrastructure development, fulfilment of basic needs of the people, expansion of industrial sector, completion of tariff and tax reform, stepping-up privatization of state-owned enterprises and adoption of locally relevant development model.

The efforts made by the Government of India towards economic globalization have attracted both positive and negative comments from the community of scholars and activists. The globalization of Indian economy has also paved the way for the globalization of Indian media. The Prime Minister has strongly pleaded that Indian media should go out and straddle the globe by carrying the country's view point to global audience saying, "We need our own CNNs and BBCs—a global Indian channel with a global perspective and reaching out to a global audience."

Impact of Foreign Direct Investment on Indian Media

Tomlinson (1999) defines globalization as complex connectivity referring to the rapidly developing and ever more complex network of interconnections and interdependencies that characterize modern social life. The process of globalization of economy has brought about series of changes over a period of time in terms of domestic and global economies. Several multi-national corporations have come into existence in various developing countries which account for almost one-third of the global stock of inward Foreign Direct Investment (FDI), compared to slightly more than one-fifth in 1990. The increased role of FDI in developing and emerging economies has raised expectations about its potential contribution to their development.

Singh (2005) noted that particularly in the field of media, telecommunication, power, retail, water and sanitation, the foreign exchange would facilitate the augmentation of balance of payment problems in host countries. The entry of FDI has also attracted serious criticism by the scholars who have accused that Multi-National Corporations (MNC) have brought about unfair competition which has resulted in low wages and labour standards abroad. In some cases, the critics have also noted that multi-national corporations have deliberately violated human and labour rights in developing countries. The importance of FDI in the world economy has increased rapidly during the last two decades. The total stock of FDI increased from 8 per cent of world GDP in 1990 to 30 per cent in 2012. The share of non-OECD countries in the global stock of inward FDI has risen from 22 per cent in 1990 to 35 per cent in 2012. The increase in FDI has been particularly pronounced in developing countries, largely reflecting the integration of large emerging economies including the so-called BRICs (Brazil, Russia, India and China), into the world economy.

In reality, the inward FDI has become the main source of external finance for developing countries and is more than twice as large as official development aid in the new millennium. The developing countries have also become more active as foreign direct investors themselves. The rise in outward FDI in emerging economies reflects predominantly the increase in FDI between non-OECD countries (South-South FDI). Outward FDI by emerging economies into the OECD remains relatively small, despite recurrent claims in the popular media that developing countries are acquiring strategic assets in OECD countries. The multi-national corporations have gained an upper hand over the domestic firms which have allowed them to compete successfully in foreign markets, despite the additional cost of having to coordinate activities across different countries.

The champions of FDI have advocated that it could be beneficial for host economies since it creates high-quality jobs, higher pay and better working conditions. The transfer of knowledge would result from worker mobility, when domestic firms recruit workers with experience in foreign firms. The increased product-market competition would strengthen incentives among domestic firms to improve their efficiency. Experience reveals that FDI did not have positive effects on the performance of local firms in India and other developing nations. This view is based on a substantial body of research using information on cross-border takeovers to identify the effects of foreign ownership on average wages within firms. In addition to having direct effects on workers employed by MNEs, FDI may also have indirect effects on workers' employment conditions in domestic firms when their knowledge spillovers associated with FDI.

The effect on workers in domestic firms, however, is considerably weaker than the direct effect on employees of foreign affiliates of multi-national corporations. Studies have also rightly revealed that FDI did not bring about any kind of expansion of the informal sector or non-compliance with labour standards. The workers in the unorganized sector have become the worst victims of the entry of FDI. The benefits of FDI are not evenly spread over the host-country population. The policy makers have not given a serious thought to the negative implications of FDI on the domestic economy in general and the workers and consumers in particular. The Better Work Programme, a joint initiative launched by the International Finance Corporation (a member of the World Bank Group) and the International Labour Organization (ILO) in 2006, is a promising initiative since it would raise the working conditions in the supply-chain factories through the enhanced public monitoring of labour practices and the provision of technical assistance and credit facilities to programme participants.

China has adopted certain effective measures which have safeguarded the economy over a period of time. It has considerably influenced the regional institutions and economic structure. The salient feature of contemporary Chinese economic growth is its high saving and investment rates, both in comparison to its past and to that in other emerging-market economies. The China's fiscal position has also remained relatively sound, with budget deficits remaining close to 3 per cent of GDP and the debt-to-GDP ratio in the vicinity of 25 per cent. Rapid expansion of export from and import into China has contributed a great deal to the sustained growth in multilateral trade. The growth rates of its exports and imports were much faster than the world average for over two decades.

Impact of Globalization on Print Media in India

The English press and vernacular press have flourished since independence in India. The Press in India played a historical role during emergency (1975-77) and sustained the democracy and freedom of speech and expression. The advertisers have found that print media are more time-efficient and effective than other media of communication. Even now, the newspapers continue to reach more people than the Internet does. The digital advertising revenues are not compensating for the advertisement revenues lost to print media. The revenue model for news companies in the social media arena remains hard to find. The news publishing business has become one of constant updating, of monitoring, distilling and repacking information, observes Shyam Parekh, editor of DNA, Ahmedabad. The print media have moved opinion and commentary to the front page while the editorial page served the purpose of the voice of the newspaper organization. The print media continue to exercise a large degree of independence on the basis of the backing of large business houses.

In India, the Express News Service, the Press Trust of India and the United News of India are among the major news agencies. There are a good number of smaller news agencies which provide constant news services. In the age of economic globalization, the government regulation of access to newsprint was liberalized. Besides this, the independence of India's press has been bolstered by the liberalization of government economic policy and the increase of private-sector advertising provided by the growth of India's private sector and the spread of consumerism. The controls on the distribution of news print could also be used to reward favoured publications and threaten those that fell into disfavour.

The major national newspapers in India include—*Times of India*, *Indian Express*, *Hindustan Times*, *The Hindu*, *Statesman*, *Tribune* and so on. The prominent regional newspapers of India include *Malayala Manorama*, *Madhyamam*, *Dainik Jagran*, *Anandabazar Patrika*, *Vijaya Karnataka*, *Prajavani*, *Kannada Prabha*, *Andhra Prabha*, *Dina Tanthi* and so on. The newspaper sale in the country increased by 12 per cent in 2012. India is also recognized as one of the largest markets in the world of newspapers followed by China and Japan. Manjula Rajagopal, associate editor of *Dinamalar* observed that print media business boomed in India in the new millennium.

Indian print media is one of the largest print media networks in the world. The English press and vernacular press have grown as the powerful fourth estate of democracy in the post-independence era. There are presently about 80,000 dailies and periodicals which are brought out in English, Hindi and other vernacular languages. The print media in India also earn revenue from circulation, advertising and job printing sources. Nobel Prize-winner Amartya Sen famously said there has never been a famine in a democratic country because the news about food shortages or distribution failures cannot be hidden and suppressed. Globalization has posed series of threats and opportunities to the print media in India. The reputation of print media is impeccable. The newspapers and magazines are managed on the basis of sound principles and practices of management.

The Indian Press witnessed series of changes after 1991. Prominent among them include—change of political economy of the press, fierce competition from the satellite television channels, increase of advertising revenue, better purchasing power of the people, improved literacy status, market driven economy, corporatization of the press, growth of vernacular press and so on. The commendable growth of language press in the 1990s was termed by Robin Jaffrey (2000) as 'Indian Newspaper Revolution'.

Ninan (2007) observes: "Hindi newspapers, harbingers of nationalism at the turn of the century, had witnessed more material change by the turn of 21st century. They bursted with contour supplement and marketing coupons even as they brought politics, sports and news to rural and urban homes." The Indian print media grew considerably in the age of globalization because of the entry of local market forces into print media in India.

The Government of India allowed 26 per cent of Foreign Direct Investment in 2002 in accordance with the policy of economic liberalization. Subsequently, the format and contents of the newspapers changed in order to overcome the competition posed by the electronic media. The print media gained advertising revenue remarkably due to 'profit over people' concept influenced by the globalization. Major newspapers created a new trend known as 'infotainment' to give news in an entertainment form and attract the young generation of readers. The editorialization of news also became a way of life in the mainstream and leading language newspapers. This tendency also enabled the multinational corporations to have a sway on knowledge of the people. The Press Council of India vehemently opposed the entry of FDI in print media due to these reasons.

Aggrawal and Gupta (2001) write: "The rapid technological changes, which the print media is adapting to survive, has brought about far-reaching changes in the contemporary media scenario. The leading newspapers are taking to online journalism in a bigway. Several leading print media organizations have been developing comprehensive websites of their own, which regularly cover interviews, chat shows, business and economy news, lifestyles and entertainment."

Consequent on entry of FDI in Indian media, the foreign contents in the Indian newspapers have increased substantially. The foreign journalists also found place in the Indian print media and championed the neo-liberalism. Some innovative experiments are made by the editors of Indian Press. The editorial pages are dropped and opposite editorial pages provide more opinions and analyses. The modern

Indian newspapers have found the new digital markets which have grown in the rural areas also. According to Mariam Mammen Mathew, Manorama Online in India, the urban youth are turning to TV, online and mobile. Indian media institutions have grown commendably over a period of time and the Indian media industry is expected to cross US$ 200 billion by 2015 according to the analysts. It reached US $ 11.92 billion mark in 2007 and is the fastest growing in the Asia-Pacific region according to the latest evidence.

The situation is quite promising for the Indian print media also since the number of publications is constantly increasing even though the print media literacy has not increased substantially in the country. The newspaper business in India is gaining 10 per cent per year. The optimists have cited certain examples with respect to the better growth of print media in India. They include—ability of the print media to provide more space for public issues, capacity of the print media for better agenda setting, credibility of the print media as informal universities, reputation of the print media as effective watch dogs of public interest, role of print media as active engagers, emergence of online journalism, development of print media organizations into multi-media platforms, increasing number of investigative and advocacy oriented writings, growth of economy and purchasing power of the people, steady increase in the literacy status of the people and so on.

In the present times, the print media are also affected by the global recession. In particular, the newspapers and magazines have been losing readers in 15-25 age categories to television and internet. The readers are also getting news freely through the growing number of news sites on net and mobile news groups. The television news channels are also providing the free news to the viewers constantly. The growth and development of user friendly social media has resulted in the increasing number of bloggers and v-loggers in the modern society. The newspaper business is gaining 10 per cent every year but the readers would prefer their news on a tablet computer.

These factors are duly considered as the major threats to the future of print media in India. Besides this, the cost of production and distribution of newspapers and periodicals is also increasing. The print media market in India is extremely price-sensitive and the status of circulation of the press naturally affects the advertisement tariff and revenue. The culture of Indian journalism is also changing due to these factors in the age of globalization. The newspapers and magazines are capable of providing in depth coverage of issues concerning the public interests when compared to television, internet and social media.

Impact of Globalization on Electronic Media in India

Radio is an effective medium of mass communication in India. Radio was developed as a prominent means of communication in the post-independence era in India. Radio is also known as inexpensive medium of communication and the actual number of listeners has absolutely no effect on production expenses. The modern web radio is also intangible and the big audiences are much more expensive for the radio operator to serve than small ones. All India Radio is the single largest broadcasting network in the world. The programme and other internally generated revenues account for between 0 per cent and 100 per cent of revenues.

The broadcasters have used certain hybrid models which govern the economics of radio. The subscription, exterior business financing, commercial sponsorship and direct advertising models are all market based or consumer dependent models, because the amount of income generated with these models is directly dependent on the quantity and quality of programme consumers. Tax funding, licence fees, exterior private financing and voluntary listener sponsorship are non-market or non-consumer dependent models, because the amount of income is not directly dependent on the quantity and quality of programme consumption. In the present times, over 95 per cent of the country's population is covered by All India Radio's broadcast services. India also has quite a large number of commercial channels.

The special audience programmes have attracted large number of children, adolescents, women, farmers, workers and other sections of society. In reality, the listenership of radio has either dropped or reached a plateau in a country like India. In the urban areas, FM stations are more popular through film and other popular music programmes. Recently, efforts are made by various organizations to empower the people through community radio programmes with a focus on development broadcasting. Community radio stations are also developed in order to facilitate decentralized and localized broadcasting services in the urban, rural and tribal areas. Modern radio takes many forms, including wireless networks and mobile communications of all types, as well as radio broadcasting. Before the advent of television, commercial radio broadcasts included not only news and music, but dramas, comedies, variety shows, and many other forms of entertainment. The community radio stations are generally less expensive to operate programming than commercial and public stations which have the potential reach of the programming from community stations. Radio City, Radio Mirchi, Big FM, Red FM and other radio channels have attracted the attention of the people in the urban areas.

Television is an electronic telecommunication medium for transmitting and receiving moving images that can be monochrome (black-and-white) or coloured, with accompanying sound. 'Television' may also refer specifically to a television set, television programming, television transmission. Doordarshan has emerged as the second largest television network in the world. There are also a good number of foreign and domestic television channels which are competing with Doordarshan in the country. In India, television has emerged as the prominent medium of mass communication. Television has reigned supreme over all the other media of mass communication on account of its inbuilt characteristics. The upheavals in the nature of Indian television have been accompanied by a simultaneous expansion in its reach and penetration.

Television has attracted large number of audiences in India regardless of gender, age, education, profession, income and other factors. Television industry has grown in India remarkably over a period of time. The broadcast television is financed by either government, advertising, licensing (a form of tax), subscription or any combination of these. The subscription TV channels are usually encrypted to ensure that only subscription payers receive the decryption codes to see the signal. There is ever growing number of television sets in India and television generates revenue through advertising, subscription fees and public funding. Television also generates adequate income through commercial broadcasting programmes.

The broad access of television makes it a powerful and attractive medium for advertisers. The modern television programmes combine varying degrees of social value with commercial appeal in a competitive market. The television in India is also targeting the specific segments of the audience, in particular, young adults. The urban, middle to upper class youth, especially, constitute a key target group for private channels. Doordarshan network consists of 64 Doordarshan Kendras/Production Centres, 24 Regional News Units, 126 Doordarshan Maintenance Centres, 202 High Power transmitters, 828 Low Power Transmitters, 351 Very Low Power Transmitters, 18 Transposes, 30 Channels and DTH Services according to the latest statistics.

In the age of globalization, there was worldwide surge of commercial television. The emergence of satellite and cable distribution of programming has dramatically increased the number of channels available in India. Throughout the world, commercialization of national television systems has become an integral part of globalization programmes. The Doordarshan's commercialization and self-financing was encouraged by the increasingly neo-liberal governments of the 1980s and 90s. A more important development was the introduction of a five channel satellite service in 1991 by Hong Kong based Star TV, eventually controlled by Rupert Murdoch. This system was well received by the Indian elite. Globalization has assisted in networking among media professionals and has revolutionized news, printing, editing and reportage. Globalization has made possible adequate and timely processing and dissemination of information through radio and television networks.

Several committees headed by legal luminaries, bureaucrats, policy-makers and intellectuals have examined the question of autonomy to electronic media in India. The broadcasting system has been reformed over a period of time on the basis of the reports submitted by various committees. The Government of India enacted the Prasar Bharati Act, 1990. The Government of India liberalized the broadcasting policy since it viewed media as one of the many sectors like steel, textile, coal and iron which indicated the influence of globalization and neo-liberalism on media.

The Sen Gupta Committee submitted its report in 1996 and suggested that the creation of Radio and Television Authority of India as an independent body outside the purview of Prasar Bharati Corporation. The Committee also suggested the extension of uplinking facilities to domestic and foreign satellite channels and bring them under the purview of Indian laws. Subsequently, All India Radio and Doordarshan were brought under the Prasar Bharathi Corporation in 1997 when S. Jaipal Reddy was the Minister for Information and Broadcasting.

There was a definite policy shift in the management of electronic media in India which was greatly influenced by the process of economic liberalization and historical Supreme Court's judgment of 1995. The Supreme Court observed that the airways should not be the monopoly of anybody in a democratic country like India. This judgment led to the creation of an autonomous body for the management of All India Radio and Doordarshan. There was a great spurt of FM stations which posed challenges to the administrators and professionals of Indian broadcasting media.

The radio and television networks are very well developed in India especially in the post-independence era. All India Radio and Doordarshan are owned, managed and controlled by the Prasar Bharati Corporation. The private radio and television channels are giving tough competition to the All India Radio and Doordarshan. The public and private radio and television networks and operations are complimented by the application of innovative broadcasting technologies and progressive techniques of broadcasting media management in India in the age of globalization.

The radio and television programmes are produced locally and relayed through local independent television stations. The programmes primarily contain songs and news from Bollywood. Most of the programmes are broadcast for few hours during the weekends and supported by local ethnic advertisers such as ethnic grocery stores, basmati rice or masala distributors, and local Hindi cinema halls. Indian programmes have been relayed in the US for some time, but they are targeted only to the expatriates from the Indian subcontinent. The India-based or UK-based Indian channels such as Zee TV, Zee Gold, Sony Asia, and B4U are attracting the audiences in large number.

The Indian television industry can follow the lead of the Australian, British, Italian, German, and French television industries in international co-production in the age of globalization through certain innovative broadcasting techniques. Prominent among them include—identification of new market opportunities, developing globally competitive broadcasting services, cultivating global mindset, delivering user-friendly broadcasting services and so on. The recent broadcasting innovations such as interactive television, high-definition television, the convergence of computing with telecasting, digital video assistants, virtual VCRs, and home theatre technologies are extending the horizons of television as an ultimate mode of entertainment and advertisement in the new millennium.

The invasion of sky by the satellite television also compelled certain major policy changes in the electronic media management in India. The Government of India liberalized the broadcasting and allowed the broadcasters irrespective of their ownership and management to uplink from India with a condition that they must abide by the norms and guidelines with respect to advertising and broadcasting codes. There was no restriction on foreign equity in production of software, marketing of television rights, airtime and advertisements. In 2005, about 58 companies were enabled to uplink 68 TV channels with varying degree of foreign equity and remaining 41 companies were permitted to uplink 93 TV channels which had 100 per cent Indian equity.

Sapna Bhatia (2002) has examined the role of Indian television in the context of marketization and globalization. She notes: "The rapid expansion of the television services has provided more entertainment and advertisement services. In the 1980s, television became a quasi-commercial medium and commercialization of Indian broadcasting increased after globalization. The Nehru-Sarabhai approach of tapping the communication revolution and television, as a major tool for the development of the masses had been ignored. The entry of foreign satellite channels eroded whatever little the national electronic media had been doing for socio-economic development in spite of the pressures of commercialization. Marketisation has changed the content and role of television from development to entertainment-oriented. Globalization has further pushed the culture of consumerism with television being the main carrier of consumer capitalism around the world."

The emergence of private television channels in India brought the television programmes to the doorsteps of the people. The new media allowed greater audience participation. There is a growing selection of satellite transmission and cable services available in India.

Competition from the satellite stations brought radical change to Akashavani and Doordarshan by cutting its audience and threatening its advertising revenues at a time when the government was pressuring it to pay for expenditures from internal revenues. The global media conglomerates have shown interest in Indian broadcasting market and launched regional television news channels. These developments have brought about an era of competitive broadcasting in India despite certain disadvantages.

Impact of Globalization on Film Media in India

The cinema is a very popular form of entertainment which has cut across all barriers. It is also a democratic medium of communication. Alexander Walker noted that film is the most influential entertainment and art form. Vilanilan records: "How the movies contributed to the democratization of communication in society is evident from the fact that all over the world it is the most common and economical entertainment for ordinary people."

The films are the most effective means of communication and indicators of the development of a country since they give something for everyone. The film is the only medium which has been classified as 'super art' since it has borrowed several inputs from painting, dance, music, theatre and photography. It has been considered as a major institution of communication because of sheer number of people depending on it for livelihood. Lenin, the architect of October Revolution in Russia had immense faith in cinema as a social communication medium. He rightly believed that cinema could play a major role as catalyst in shaping the society. The Eastern European countries were also greatly influenced by the power of cinema and established film institutes to train the people in the art and craft of film making.

The Lumiere brothers began an innings of film exhibition in India in 1895 at Bombay. Ardeshir Irani became the first producer and director of film in India through the release of '*Alam Ara*' on March 14, 1931. In the decade of 1930s, the film as a medium of communication gained popularity in India and about 1,000 films in various languages were produced annually. India emerged as a prominent film making country in the world. Statistically speaking, India produces largest number of newsreels, documentaries and feature films in the world.

Since beginning, the cinema has been a profit-oriented business enterprise in India. As the film industry gained new dimensions, the producers came in large number and produced commercial films on the basis of box office economics. Barnow and Krishnamurthy (1980) recall: "With black market and corruption abounding in the country, businessman began to think in terms of easy money and quick returns. The inflationary war boom has been greatest encouragement for all and sundry to enter the various branches of the film industry in India." The Hollywood also gained a foothold in India with special effects films such as Jurassic Park (1993) and Speed (1994) which were appreciated by the Indian audiences.

The Bollywood continued to be formula based story lines, expertly choreographed fight scenes, spectacular song and dance routines, emotion-charged melodrama, and larger-than-life heroes in the world. The Government of India established the National Film Development Corporation (NFDC) in order to promote healthy film culture and production in India. Subsidized financial assistance was given to the producers of new wave cinema in India. A good number of award winning new wave films were produced by the talented and committed Indian film makers. This measure certainly enabled the Indian film industry to improve the quality of film making but also helped the industry to grow in a healthy and robust manner.

Thoraval (2000) states: "India is one of the rare examples of a non-Western country where cinema was not simply confined to metropolis but penetrated to rural areas as well. The Indian public both in the cities and countryside consists of some of the most avid enthusiastic movie goers to be found in the world." The adventurous and enterprising film makers also explored the foreign market.

Kohli (2006) pointed out that Indian films attracted the Indian Diaspora and earned adequate foreign exchange rates than the previous years. The Indian films earned more revenue from overseas than in India in the age of globalization. The Indian film industry witnessed an upsurge of new wave films in the decades of 1970s, 1980s and 1990s.

The Indian film industry had lost its audience to the video clubs and video theatres in 1980s. The invasion of Indian sky by the satellite television also adversely affected the business prospects of Indian film industry. Khandekar (2006) reports: "Till the mid 80s, films had for worse—a captive audience. After the decline of Amitabh Bachchan, there was no other major star on the horizon who could attract both financiers and audiences. Video and Cable TV cut the time a film had to recover its most in the theatres—to less than half. The cost of film production became very high by 1993, this figure had gone upto 30-50 million. As viewers started hooked to soaps, there was no need to spend a lot of money on films. The satellite channels began buying under production rights or libraries. These developments, combined with alterations in policy, finally forced some structural changes in the film industry."

The digital technology, multiplex and PRV theatres also sprung up in metros and motivated the audience to see a good number of bollywood and regional films. India has emerged as a prominent film making country in the world. The film field is blessed with internationally reputed directors, artistes and technicians. The film as a medium gained popularity in the country as many as 1,000 films in various languages of India are produced annually. The bollywood and regional cinema have grown commendably over a period of time in India.

The country has produced creative and qualitative films which have earned international recognition. The Films Division of India produces largest news reels and documentaries which have focused the attention of the audience on vital issues concerning national development. The film makers have adopted the state-of-the-art technologies and tested techniques of film making and brought reputation for the Indian film industry in the age of globalization.

The Indian film industry was affected by several trends and developments in the age of globalization. The satellite channels such as Sony or Zee paid high prices for films in 1990s. As the reach and power of television increased, the hit films could do more on both counts-TRPs and revenues. The satellite channels also began buying under-production rights or libraries. The bidding for films reached the terrific height in the new millennium. The result costs spiralled from an average Rs.50 million in 1999 to a whopping Rs. 100-150 million for making the big budget film.

The foreign companies entered the Indian film market for the distribution of local films in 2001 on a commission basis. Some Indian companies forayed into music, home video, international and domestic distribution of films. The multiplexes, digital theatres and home video became three major sources of entertainment. The sheer permutations and combinations that a multiplex offers—to mix films, shows, timings and prices—made it easier to make money.

The current entertainment tax policy of the government has enabled the multiplexes to make about 70 per cent gross margins. If multiplexes are changing film viewing patterns in the cities, the digital theatres are changing them in smaller towns and rural areas. This has added a pan-Indian flavour to the changes sweeping across film retail in India. The digital technology and digital theatre have added new dimension to film industry in India. The home video market also grew considerably in India since the prices of home video rights range from Rs.0.5 million to Rs.10 million.

The Indian film industry has undergone sweeping changes in the age of globalization. The film industry has also welcomed the media conglomerates which have integrated the process of film making—from ideation to music, to production and distribution across the world. This tendency has made it easier to capture the value of movies through ownership of rights for music, television, home video, overseas and so on. The economics of film industry has changed due to the domination of leading national and international companies. The overseas market has grown up considerably.

Impact of Globalization on New Communication Technologies in India

The new media have grown considerably in India. The new media have been rightly considered as the instruments of development by the scholars all over the world. The Government of India have formulated the new media policy in order to facilitate expansion, decentralization and democratization of new media in the Indian Republic. The policy makers have realized that active participation of underprivileged, marginalized, underserved and under-represented segments of society, including women and weaker sections is very crucial from the point of view of inclusive development. India is heading in the right direction with the development of new media in modern society. The telecommunication, satellite communication and computer communication technological applications constitute the gamut of 'new media' in modern society. Modern government and non-government organizations have utilized the new media for developmental endeavours in all spheres of human life.

The Tata Consultancy Services—established in 1968 by the Tata Group—were the country's largest software producers during the 1960s. The Indian Government acquired the EVS EM computers from the Soviet Union, which were used in large companies and research laboratories. The 'microchip revolution' of the 1980s had convinced both Indira Gandhi and her successor Rajiv Gandhi that electronics and telecommunications were vital to India's growth and development. Sam Pitroda brought about commendable telecom revolution in India under the leadership of Rajiv Gandhi. Abdul Kalam, U.R. Rao, Kasturi Rangan, Madhavan Nambiyar and others developed India as a satellite communication power in the world. India also became a prominent power in the field of computer application since the Indian Government created three wide-area computer networking schemes in the 1980s, namely—INDONET (intended to serve the IBM mainframes in India), NICNET (network for the National Informatics Centre), and the academic research oriented Education and Research Network (ERNET).

The liberalization of Indian economy in 1991 under the dynamic leadership of P.V. Narasimha Rao and Manmohan Singh brought about remarkable economic growth of over 6 per cent annually during 1993-2002. The economic reforms were driven in part by significant application of new media in India. The National Democratic Alliance Government led by Atal Bihari Vajpayee accorded high priority for the development of new media in India. The Government formed the Indian National Task Force on Information Technology and Software Development in 1996. India achieved series of developments in the fields of telecommunication, satellite communication and computer communication by the end of the 20th century. The BSNL, Bharti Airtel, Reliance Communications, Vodafone and other organizations became the prominent institutions which played a crucial role in the telecom revolution in India.

The Central Government also prepared solid grounds for the development of e-governance in the country through several initiatives towards application of ICT at various stages of development/ implementation of Central Government which includes—India Portal,

National Institute of e-governance, central repository of data, dissemination of information relating to best practices/innovations in e-governance, awards for best websites and innovative use of IT in the delivery of public services. The citizen service centres were set up for one stop and non-stop delivery of services to the public. The India Portal is a user-friendly portal of all government web sites for providing information and delivery of services on the policies and programmes of the government. Several state governments also launched innovative steps to promote e-governance across the country. Andhra Pradesh, Madhya Pradesh, Rajasthan and Karnataka emerged as model states in the application of new media for development purposes.

The basis of the information revolution in India is the technological revolution in telecommunications, computers and electronic media. There has been a convergence of technologies relating to different areas of communication such as telephone, telegraph, radio, TV, Internet and data networks. The process of globalization has facilitated greater potential benefit of information and communication technologies. India has become an information/data processing service provider to the world. In India, telecommunication has become a substitute for transport as the information collection role of transport is minimized due to information flows which are efficient and cost effective. The technological advances have made possible the unbundling of telecom services in India. The market based approach has been accepted and implemented in India which is known for investment de-licensing and free entry, rational pricing of natural resource, regulation of quasi-natural monopoly elements and tax and subsidy for social objectives.

In India, the emergence of cable TV and wireless technology has brought about the natural monopoly position which has urban and rural utility. The government has complete authority over all physical channels of communication including television and radio broadcast. The social concerns are met through a cross tax subsidy scheme. There is no economic rationale for any licence fees and charges on account of full cost pricing of all telecom services in India.

India has become a prominent nation in the world for the development and application of new communication technologies which have become effective instruments of education and development. Eminent communication scholars and scientists have prepared grounds for the conduction of new media experiments in the country. India is in the forefront in the field of new media management in the world and conducted several experiments in the field of application of new media for various developmental endeavours during the last quarter of 20th century. In the present times, the social media have also become prominent tools of multi-faceted development of the country on the basis of interactive and democratized communication in urban and rural areas. The communication and information specialists have adopted the best strategies for the effective management of new media for various developmental activities in the age of globalization.

Impact of Globalization on Folk Media in India

Globalization is a term that came into popular usage in the 1980s to describe the increased movement of people, knowledge and ideas, and goods and money across national borders that has led to increased interconnectedness among the world's populations, economically, politically, socially and culturally. Although globalization is often thought of in economic terms (the global marketplace), this process has many social, cultural and political implications as well. Many in local communities associate globalization with modernization (i.e. the transformation of 'traditional' societies into 'Western' industrialized ones). At the global level, globalization is thought of in terms of the challenges it poses to the role of governments in international affairs and the global economy.

Mohanty *et al.* (2002) observe: "The tradition has played an important role in creating artistic process, particularly in the field of folk performing arts in a pluralistic society like India. Tradition is the process of transmission of the age old values and the contextual manifestation and interpretation of the universe. The traditional performing arts indicate belongingness and affinity in cultural context and are considered as an integral part of general life of people in traditional societies. The first significant international recognition of the traditional media in the communication and development strategies of the developing countries which was recognized by the international parenthood federation and UNESCO sponsored conferences in the early 1970s."

Chiovoloni (2004) stated that folk media or local or traditional communication systems refer to organized processes of production and exchange of information managed by rural communities. These include traditional theatre or dramas, masks and puppet performances, tales, proverbs, riddles and songs. They are cultural and endogenous responses to different community needs for information, education, social protest and entertainment.

The folk media have grown along with the culture and traditions of India. They have undergone a tremendous subjective change from mythology to onslaught of socio-politico-economical changes. The folk artists have used creative methods to facilitate the active participation of the audience. The impact of globalization on culture has become a debatable issue. As a matter of fact, the cultural identity is part and parcel of national identity.

The folk media are also known as traditional or indigenous media which are deep rooted in the Indian culture. They are the communities' own channels which are more simple, effective and credible for diffusing messages to the audience in their own language. The traditional performing arts are woven in the lives of the people of India. The folk media have a direct contact with the audience. The treatment of message is completely determined by them in terms of degree of effectiveness in emphasizing the message and impact of messages on the audience. "The folk media are also primary channels of communication to the under privileged communities of India. The audience accept the messages which are imparted through the medium of their own culture according to the past studies", notes Varsha Das (1992).

The process of globalization and media imperialism have brought about the replacement of endogenous cultures across the globe. Some argue that the local cultures have the capacity to resist the globalizing trends. Kiran Ramachandran Nair (1997) has examined the relationship between the culture and social pluralism in India. She writes: "India is acclaimed over the world as one of the most socially complex, culturally diverse and pluralistic country. The composite culture of India is characterized by a remarkable capacity for assimilation and synthesis of various streams of thought and ideas. Pluralism is believed to contribute positively to the ability of individuals to function in a participative society. Secularism as a harmonizing philosophy tries to forge a comprehensive universal spirit of integration among the people of India characterized by religious, linguistic and cultural pluralism."

The most significant development in the context of globalization is Information and the Communication Technology (ICT) influx. It converted the world into a global village. In a democratic country like India marked by the diversity of languages and culture greater value is attached to ICT for the development of rural sector. The folk media are very powerful tools of communication among the indigenous people of India since they are equivalent of exogenous mass media which facilitate communication among the rural mass for socio-economic growth and development.

The impact of globalization on local culture and the changing role of the nation-state can be examined by observing the particularities of the social and cultural patterns and their local, national and transnational manifestations in India. These social and cultural realities have a plural character in terms of language, geography, ethnicity, religion and culture. With partial exception of the tribal population, the caste system and its related kinship structures have shaped the profile of the culture, economy and power-structures within the local communities and regions.

Kamlongera and Van Den Stichele (2000), Zwaal (2000), Panford *et al.* (2001), Adoyo (2004) and other scholars have examined the relevance of folk media in the developing countries. They have reported that many rural people utilized folk media for communication of cultural messages. Chauhan (2004) advocated that policy makers involved in planning and implementation of research and extension activities of agricultural fields should use the combinations of traditional and electronic extension methods, make available rural agricultural libraries and facility of Internet at village level.

Broadly speaking, folk media or traditional media include folk songs, folk dance, folk theatre and folk traditions in a developing country like India. Especially, the folk theatre forms or dramas are very effective means of educating the rural and tribal people. Penelist and Adoyo (2004) defined drama as a traditional means of information which allow different possible endings by encouraging audience participation which is aimed at changing the behaviour of participants of such means of communication. In a developing country like India, an effective communication system of folk media along with mass media is an essential element in modernizing the rural and tribal people who are excluded from the mainstream of national life.

The social and cultural realities have a plural character in terms of language, geography, ethnicity, religion and culture. With partial exception of the tribal population, the caste system and its related kinship structures have shaped the profile of the culture, economy and power-structures within the local communities and regions, according to the survey conducted by the Anthropological Survey of India (1998). The study also revealed that the ethnography, which is marked by endogamy, occupation and perception is threatened by globalization.

The advent of new media in the age of globalization has adversely affected the folk media which have become non-entities on account of cultural imperialism. Boyd-Barrett (1997) writes that the country which is affected by media influence either adopts this influence as a deliberate commercial or political strategy, or simply absorbs this influence unreflectively as the result of the contract. Herbert Schiller (1976) comments: "The concept of cultural imperialism today best describes the sum of the processes by which a society is brought into the modern world system and how is dominating stratum is attracted, pressured, forced, and sometimes bribed into shaping social institutions to correspond to, or even promote, the value and structures of the dominating centre of the system."

The folk media in India are used as supplements to the mass media rather than at the centre of communication efforts to reach 70 per cent of India's total population who live in villages. The traditional performing arts are functional, interpersonal and contextual by nature and represent the cultural milieu of the country. The traditional media became effective in many political and social campaigns launched by Mahatma Gandhi. Likewise, the eminent Tamil poet Sumbramanium Bharati started using folk music to evoke patriotic feelings. Folk tunes were used to popularize songs and glories of spinning wheels and consequently boycotting British goods. In 1940s, Indian People Theatre Association effectively used some theatre forms like '*Jatra*' of Bengal, '*Bhavai*' of Gujarat, '*Tamasha*' of Maharashtra, '*Burrakatha*' of Andhra Pradesh, to create political awareness among the people and enlist their active participation in the mainstream politics.

Kamla (2004) emphasized the need for community social workers to understand the rudiments of indigenous communication. Moreover, this becomes realistic when considered that indigenous people are often favourably disposed to development initiatives when the changes advocated have a minimal understanding of their language, music, cultural and religious beliefs.

The process of cultural influence proceeded so subtly, without any blood being shed and with the receiving culture thinking it had sought such cultural influence. The culture-specific folk media in India have become weak and vulnerable over a period of time. Scholars have strongly criticized the process of homogenization which has weakened the foundations of folk media. According to Golding and Harris (1997), media Imperialism which is a bi-product of globalization overstates external determinants and undervalues the internal dynamics, not least those of resistance, within dependent societies. It conflates economic power and cultural effects. In India and other developing nations, cultural imperialism has caused a strong blow to the local culture including folk media.

In a developing country like India, the cultural imperialism has not spread modernity. Since it is based on false cultural consciousness which has adversely affected the local culture and culture-specific folk media in India. The process of hybridization includes the fusing, mixing, intermingling, combining, fusion and mélange of cultural forms which have belittled the cultural foundations of folk media which have served as informal universities of mankind in India since times immemorial.

The folk media have served the needs of state and society in several ways as prominent tools of education, entertainment, organization and development especially in the rural and tribal areas. The scholars have also examined the impact of globalization on folk media in India and noted that the market forces have promoted certain images of folk which are marketed not only to members of the nation, but also to tourists and outsiders attracted by the exotic and the distinct cultural products. The folk media tend to be appealing because they stimulate the senses of people by communicating several things through songs, dances, stories and other contents which have become important elements in identity formation.

Scholars have viewed globalization not just as an economic

phenomenon, but also as one that touches on all aspects of social, political, economic and cultural lives of the people in a pluralistic society like India. They have examined the impact of global forces on the local culture and folk media. The folk media specialists have also highlighted the value of creativity in folk media in their writings. Studies have revealed that the audience with a strong interest in the cultural ethos of folk media has the opportunity to expand their knowledge in a way that is not usually emphasized in the media controlled by the market forces.

Scholars have also argued that the cultural and emotional bonds are strengthened due to their global reach through new telecommunication linkages, e.g. video-meetings, tele-discussions, etc. The new media also creates 'virtual' communities and cultural enclaves by offering the possibility of sustained communicative interaction among members scattered in far off places. The television and Internet are identified by them as prominent sources which have offered a culture of information, pleasure and relative autonomy, all of which are particularly appealing to young people in India and other developing nations. In reality, many young people are simultaneously experiencing life within the global and local spheres. They may develop a global consciousness yet still have to function and survive in their own locality and culture.

The contemporary revolution in communication technology has had a dramatic impact in the arena of popular culture since the new media have enabled a wide diversity of locally-based popular culture to develop and reach a larger audience cutting across the geographical and cultural boundaries. The folk traditions of India are widely popularized among the external audience through electronic media and new media services to some extent. But, the globalization has invariably increased the transmission of Western popular culture from the developed countries to the developing countries like India. The local critics of this trend lament not only the resulting silencing of domestic cultural expression, but also the hegemonic reach of Western, 'alien' culture and the potential global homogenization of values and cultural taste which have sidelined the Indian folk media. The traditional folk media forms, once a favourite for communication efforts, are today precariously placed on account of media imperialism which is created by globalization of economy.

Boro (2006) examined the relationship between the globalization and local cultures with reference to North-East India and observed that ethnic designs, forms and products were popularized by the media. The scholar also noted that intervention from outside has put the preservation of tradition under tremendous stress, for such an intervention from the world of fashion technology will definitely transform the traditional designs, colours and forms and also their use. The study revealed that local culture and folk traditions were threatened by the outside players in modern society.

According to Levis (2002), the local people have found it difficult to preserve their local cultural character and folk music, dance and theatre forms since they could not fit into the global context. The folk media forms in India have serious limitations outside the country in view of their cultural ethos, linguistic barrier and other compulsions of modern entertainment industry in the present times.

Mohanty *et al.* (2002) noted that folk and traditional media are indeed powerful tools for rural development in India. The scholars observed that the tradition which is the cumulative social heritage in the form of habit, custom, attitude and the way of life is transmitted from generation to generation either through written words or words of mouth. The scholars further cautioned that folk media should not be allowed to perish in the age of globalization because of commercialization of culture and media services.

There are heated debates about globalization and its impact on the local culture, economy, media and audience. There are limited advantages of globalization educationally and economically with reference to India and other developing nations. But there are several threats to local culture and folk media. The scholars have identified the threats to the folk media in the age of globalization in their investigations and writings. The cultural manifestations of globalization are widely debated across the country. The industrial development brought with it social dislocations that necessitated state intervention for the rejuvenation of folk media in India. The new millennium has witnessed an internationalization of information services involving the exponential expansion of computer-based communication through the Internet and electronic mail. These new services have belittled the status of folk media in several ways in India.

Impact of Globalization on Corporate Advertising in India

Advertising industry is a rapidly growing industry and determines to a considerable extent the Gross Domestic Product (GDP) of any country. The advertising industry besides functioning as an intermediate between the manufacturers and the customers plays an important role in the Indian economy. Modern advertising industry necessitates investment for funding different resources. One cannot measure the degree of development by interpretation of inputs in the economy which yields some production. In the event when consumption levels far exceed than what is reckoned, this is not a means of triggering or bringing about transformation in the culture, society or development in human resources or economy.

The Indian corporate sector primarily depends upon advertising in order to enhance the salability of goods and services and generate adequate income in the age of competitive business. The corporate houses have invested adequate funds on corporate advertising management which is an important component of organizational management. There are about 500 leading corporate houses which are functioning in India. The corporate advertising services are delivered by the consumer goods producing corporate houses and non-consumer goods producing corporate houses. The Reserve Bank of India's (1985) has classified the industries on the basis of certain parameters.

The corporate houses mainly undertake the management of corporate advertising in respect of consumer goods as compared to non-consumer goods manufactured by them. The non-consumer goods producers included the companies producing intermediate goods as well. According to the RBI classification, the consumer goods and non-consumer goods producing companies are usually classified on the basis of the extent of foreign holding in their equity capital. The companies having 10 per cent or more foreign equity are considered to be Foreign Controlled Companies (FCCs) according to Biswajit Dhar. These included the FCCs both registered and not registered under the Monopolies and Restrictive Trade Practices Act (MRTPA). The non-Foreign Controlled Companies include both registered and non-registered under the Act.

A comprehensive study on the corporate advertising management in India was undertaken by Chalapati Rao (1990). The study revealed that about 400 corporate houses constituted the top crust of the corporate advertising management in India. The private sector has gained an upper hand over the public sector in regard to the investment made on corporate advertising activities. But, these private corporate houses did not report advertisement expenditure as a separate item in their Annual Reports. The number of companies, reporting advertisement expenditure as a separate entry, fell from 210 in 1976 to 193 in 1984 according to the study. The private corporate houses which have not reported their corporate advertising expenditure include DCM, WIMCO, Mafatlal, Parke Davis, Geoffrey Manners, General Electric Company of India and many others. Each one of them is a well-known advertiser and yet, under one or the other technical reason these companies have not reported any advertisement expenditure. The same trend continues to exist in the present times also due to inadequate advertising regulations in India.

The advertisement expenditure of private and public corporate houses has grown considerably over a period of time mainly because of the competitive business environment created in the era of globalization. By the end of 1990s, the sales turnover registered a growth of 154.77 per cent, and the advertisement expenditure registered a growth of 196.90 per cent. The sales turnover registered a growth rate of 19.35 per cent per annum, while the corresponding growth rate for the advertisement expenditure was 24.60 per cent. The amount spent on consumer goods promotion is substantially higher than the amount spent on non-consumer goods promotion in India.

Empirical evidence also reveals that the corporate advertising expenditure is related to the size of the company's turnover. The corporate houses have generally reported the advertisement expenditure which is less than 1 per cent of their sales turnover. The ratio of the advertisement expenditure to the sales turnover has also risen from 0.64 in 1976 to 0.96 in 2012. This steady rise in the ratio is an indication of the growing importance of advertising in Indian corporate sector. Studies have also reported that the advertisement sales ratio rose more sharply for the consumer goods producing companies than the non-consumer goods producing companies, standing at the level of nearly 1.00 per cent in 1976 to 1.62 per cent in 2010. The advertisement to sales ratio was higher for the FCCs than for the Indian companies and the highest for the consumer goods producing Foreign Controlled Companies (FCCs). By and large, a majority of the corporate houses have reported an yearly advertising budget of nearly half a crore of rupees till now.

The Indian corporate houses are greatly influenced by the economic globalization which has motivated the corporate houses to spend more than ₹ 1 crore on advertising. Prominent among them include—Hindustan Lever Ltd. (₹ 2.98 crore), Rallis India Ltd. (₹ 1.29 crore), Union Carbide (India) Ltd. (₹ 1.22 crore), and Peico Electronics and Electricals Ltd. (₹ 1.12 crore) and it is interesting to note that all four of them were FCCs. By 1980, the eleven companies spending more than ₹1.00 crore included seven FCCs and four Indian companies. The seven FCCs were Hindustan Lever Ltd., Glaxo Laboratories (I) Ltd., I.T.C. Ltd., Peico Electronics and Electricals Ltd., Dunlop (I) Ltd. and Richardson Hindustan Ltd. The four Indian companies who joined these FCCs were Reliance Industries Ltd., Grasim Industries Ltd., Jay Engineering Works Ltd., and Mohan Meakin Ltd., Bombay Dyeing Manufacturing Co. Ltd.

The advertisement expenditure of the top advertisers seems to have jumped in a very significant manner. The Hindustan Lever Ltd., Reliance Industries Ltd. and Food Specialities Ltd. Companies have spent more than ₹ 10 crore on the corporate advertising activities by the end of 20th century. The non-consumer goods companies which have spent more than ₹ 1 crore annually on corporate advertising include—Kirloskar Oil Engines Ltd., Tata Engineering and Locomotive Co. Ltd., Greaves Cotton and Co. Ltd., Advani Oerlikon Ltd., National Organic Chemical Industries Ltd., Nirlon Synthetic Fibres and Chemical Ltd., and MRF Ltd., Dunlop (I) Ltd. and so on.

The top corporate houses of India with reference to corporate advertising expenditure include—Hindustan Lever Ltd., Reliance Industries Ltd., Food Specialities Ltd., Peico Electronics & Electricals Ltd, ITC Ltd., Union Carbide (I) Ltd., Escorts Ltd., Glaxo Laboratories (I) Ltd., Dunlop India Ltd., Jay Engineering Works Ltd., Grasim Industries Ltd., Crompton Greaves Ltd., Bombay Dyeing & Mfg. Co. Ltd., Richardson Hindustan Ltd., Bata India Ltd., Blow Plast Ltd., Herbertsons Ltd., Modi Rubber Ltd., Reckitt & Colman of (I) Ltd., Tube Investment of (I) Ltd., Johnson & Johnson Ltd., VST Industries Ltd., Raymond Woollen Mills Ltd., Voltas Ltd., Boots Co. of India Ltd., Berger Paints India Ltd., Modi Spinning and Wvg Mills

Co. Ltd., Hoechst India Ltd., Mohan Meakin Ltd., M.R.F. Ltd., Hindustan Ciba-Giegy Ltd., Bayer India Ltd., National Radio & Electronics Co Ltd., Rallis India Ltd,. Madura Coats Ltd., Bajaj Auto Ltd, Khatau Makanji Spg & Wvg Mills Co Ltd., Nirlon Synthetic Fibres & Chemicals Ltd., National Organic Chemicals Inds. Ltd., Mahindra & Mahindra Ltd., Breaves Cotton & Co. Ltd., Advani Oerlikon Ltd., Oriental Carpet Mfrs. Pvt. Ltd., Sylvania & Laxman Ltd., Goodlass Nerolac Paints Ltd., Alembic Chemical Works Co. Ltd,. Nicholas Laboratories India Ltd.; Tata Engineering & Locomotive Co. Ltd., Widia India Ltd., Kirloskar Electric Co. Ltd., Asian Paints India Ltd. and so on. Some more corporate houses like Wipro, Infosys, L&T etc. have joined the bandwagon of leading corporate houses which have made their presence felt in the field of corporate advertising management in India in the New Millennium.

Ranganath (2011) observes: "A perusal of the recent trends and developments of corporate advertising in India reveals very interesting findings. Prominent among them include—(a) Corporate advertising has grown considerably over a period of time in India because of economic globalization, (b) Corporate advertising in India is primarily a phenomenon of the consumer goods producing companies rather than non-consumer goods producing companies, (c) FCCs single handedly accounted for a dominant share in the total advertisement expenditure, (d) Indian Big business, as represented by the Indian MRTP companies, accounted for a sizeable share in the total advertisement budgets of the corporate sector, (e) Consumer goods producing FCCs accounted for more than four-fifths of the expenditure by the FCCs, and more than half the expenditure by the total reporting companies, (f) Definite correlation existed between the proportion of sales turnover and advertising expenditure, (g) Corporate advertisement expenditure by the Indian Corporate Sector is highly concentrated, (h) Top 50 advertisers accounted for nearly 80 per cent of the total advertisement budgets, whereas the Top 10 advertisers accounted for nearly 40 per cent of the total advertisement budgets, (i) Top 50 advertisers were primarily the consumer goods producers and the majority of them were FCCs, and (j) Hindustan Lever Ltd., the all time top advertiser accounted for nearly 10 per cent of the expenditure by the corporate sector in India."

Alan Rusbridger, the editor of the *Guardian*, a British newspaper, told an audience of Indians that digital technology was mauling the traditional print newspaper. That is certainly true in rich countries. But since 2005 the number of paid for Indian daily newspaper titles has surged by 44 per cent to 2,700, according to the World Association of Newspapers. That gives India more paid for newspapers than any other country. As of now, there are only 7 per cent of Indians surf the web regularly. "It's no threat yet," says Bharat Bhushan, the editor of the *Mail Today*, a joint venture between the *Daily Mail* (another British paper) and *India Today*, an Indian weekly.

The headlong growth of Indian newspapers is driven by rising literacy and a booming economy. The modern organizations are banking on newspaper advertisements for property, mobile phones, cars and matchmaking services. In 2012, the amount spent on newspaper advertising in India exceeded 30 per cent, the swiftest increase in the Asia-Pacific region, according to Nielsen India, a market-research firm. The television is also prominently used as an important tool of corporate advertising in the present times in India.

In the present times, corporate houses, government organizations and non-government organizations have considered corporate advertising as an important tool of corporate reputation management. Among advertising revenues, 15 to 20 per cent is kept by the number one contextual network, Google. Most large viewers view online display advertising as nothing more than traditional advertising but with the capability of customizing space for individual viewers. The transaction costs between advertiser and publisher in this case is 20 per cent more than the sales price after taking into account publisher tools and advertisement networks, much higher than the costs of intermediation in other kinds of industries.

Impact of Globalization on Corporate Communication in India

The British Institute of Public Relations defined the function of Public Relations which is now vigorously practiced as Corporate Communication as an effort to establish and maintain mutual understanding between an organization and its publics. Modern organizations cannot achieve their goals in the absence of active and willing participation of various stakeholders in their affairs.

Corporate Communication is not merely confined to that of presenting the points of view of the organization but to prevail upon the leaders of the organization to reconcile or adjust in the public interest those aspects of corporate behaviour which have a social significance.

Today, political parties, religious institutions, cultural organizations, voluntary organizations, education institutions, business organizations, industrial organizations, trade unions, government organizations, NGOs—all need systematic and sustainable Public Relations activities which are now broadly practiced as Corporate Communication. The tools of Corporate Communication include—publicity, propaganda, lobbying, advertising, persuasion, etc.

Globalization of Indian economy has resulted in the entry of multinational corporations which enjoyed abundant market scope in India. Rapid expansion of Indian economy in general and public and private undertakings in particular took place with the entry of multinational corporations. These undertakings evolved and introduced new concepts of management of which Corporate Communication is an important dimension.

Following Fayol and Taylor's principles of scientific management, the emphasis shifted to maximizing productivity and competitiveness by optimizing the utilization of capital resources and human resources. Effective Human Resources Management (HRM) started with Elton Mayo's Human Relations thought which put a greater emphasis on organizational communication. A new discipline called Corporate Communication emerged on account of rapid strides in economy, management and information technology which necessitated greater research in this area. In this context, organizational management and Corporate Communication forms an inevitable link among the corporate body and constituent publics.

The fast changing economy in general and media scenario in particular have had decisive impact on corporate communication in India. The once powerful opinion leaders or community leaders are replaced by the community of corporate communicators who are well versed in the art and craft of image building, reputation management, crisis management and other aspects of corporate communication in the new millennium. Corporate communication plays a major role in facilitating constant interaction between the corporate houses and various stakeholders of organizational development in modern society.

The need for self-expression is inevitable in the present times in all modern organizations in the age of globalization. Corporate Communication helps establish a mutually beneficial relationship between the management and employees on the one hand and between the organization and stakeholders on the other hand. In a world that constantly grows complex, sophisticated and even bigger, the need for two-way persuasive Corporate Communication becomes more inevitable in the modern society. In a democratic society, the constituent publics have a right to information, right to participation, right to agitation and right to empowerment. Hence, Corporate Communication provides opportunities for meaningful dialogue between the government and people in general and between modern organizations and various stakeholders in particular. The harmonious functioning of government and corporate houses demands organized Corporate Communication.

Summary

Shashi Kumar (2007) examined the impact of globalization on Indian media. He observes: "This fatal attraction of the market and the consequent alienation from the civil society has serious implications for the future of the media themselves, although in India the freedom of and for the media are not specifically stipulated in the constitution. They are derivative right by Article 19 in the fundamental rights guaranteeing freedom of speech and expression. Quotes have repeatedly reconfirmed this right and civil society has stood shoulder to shoulder with the media whenever they were under threat whether from the executive, legislature or judiciary."

The media institutions have grown in India remarkably over a period of time. A section of scholars have argued that globalization has given new dimension to the growth and development of communications media in India. Others have noted the impact of globalization on Indian culture, tradition and media environment. They have noted that reckless liberalization of economy and hyper competitions in the media have not served any good purpose. In reality, globalization and neo-liberalism have ultimately ended in propagating neo-liberal economic policies in the country. Consequently, the media have created a consumerist society in India since they are governed by the whims and fancies of multi national corporations which are least bothered about the local culture, environment and public interest. The globalization of mass media in India possess a vide range of questions which need to be answered by enlightened community of policy makers, researchers, professionals and intellectuals.

5

Indian Communication Policy

Introduction

The globalization of media has posed series of challenges to the policy makers and professionals in India. It is a continuation of Western imperialism led by America in the new millennium. The Indian media have changed enormously from people centred profession to business oriented industry. The advent of new communication technologies has brought about the globalization of economy as well as knowledge in the present times. The media are required to play the role as the voice of the people and angel guardian of public interest in a developing country like India. The media professionals are replaced by the media executives in the age of globalization. The media institutions have also become tools of profit making to the multinational corporations. Scholars and activists have criticized the functioning of Indian media in the age of globalization. A country like India with democratic system cannot have the luxury of free and irresponsible media. If the media institutions fail to regulate themselves in accordance with the constitutional obligations and norms of social responsibility, they have to be regulated by the government. The policy makers are responsible for evolving certain checks and balances in order to safeguard the local culture, environment, value system, economy, media and public interest. Hence, formulation of national communication policy at this juncture becomes highly imperative in India. In this section, the Gandhian communication philosophy, Ambedkar's communication philosophy, Indian communication policy formulation and mission and the future of communication media in India are explored.

Gandhian Communication Philosophy

Gandhi drew his model from *Bhagavadgita*, *Upanishads* and other Indian religious scriptures and folk cultures. He created a new style of communicating with the masses and eventually inducted them into the political culture. He also created significant meanings in his messages and conveyed a new egalitarian ethics for political relationships and mass participation. The meaning conveyed was a product of social activity and the idiom used was an individual symbol which became a powerful tool for mass communication.

The term '*Ram Raj*' was used to project Gandhi's concept of a welfare society. Gandhi's explained it thus: "Ram Raj is the kingdom of righteousness. By Ram Raj I do not mean Hindu Raj. I mean by Ram Raj Divine Raj, the kingdom of god. Other symbolic expressions and idioms, namely *Charkha* (spinning wheel), *Khadder* (hand-spun cloth), *Daridra Narayan* (the poorest of the poor), *Harijan* (children of god), *Satyagraha* (struggle for truth and justice), *Swadeshi* (locally manufactured goods and services), *Gram Swaraj* (rural independence), *Gramin Vikas* (rural development), *Swavalamban* (self-reliance), etc., were rooted in the socio-cultural experiences of the masses and stimulated inter-personal communications in India.

Gandhian model helped influence the attitudes of the people and build a national movement for the attainment of freedom. The channels of communication for the dissemination of his ideas were traditional and inter-personal communication tools such as *bhajans* (prayer meetings), discourses (public lectures), processions (peace marches), demonstrations (truthful and non-violent opposition), agitations (peaceful and non-violent struggles), etc. He also edited *Young India*, *Harijan*, *Navjeevan* and *Indian Opinion* which brought about tremendous awareness among the masses in India and abroad.

Mass communication does not occur only through the use of big media or new technology especially at the grassroots level in a developing country like India. The policy makers must realize that India needs simple, low-cost, innovative, credible and participatory communication media and approaches which can meet the local needs of development. The communication policy makers have to look into the traditional media of communication, inter-personal channels and non-government organizations which are rooted in the culture of Indian society.

Gandhi rejected the transformation of our higher culture into material culture. His system of communication was rooted in the Indian tradition and needs. He used his model of communication and development to solve the problems of the people very effectively. In view of this, Gandhi's attempts at public education, organization and development may be considered a hold over from the past. On the other hand, Gandhian participatory 'Sarvodaya Model of Communication and Development' can be an effective instrument of grassroots development in India. The policy makers must give a serious thought to Gandhian communication policy and model and re-design the national communication system towards realizing the dream of Gandhi in the age of globalization.

Ambedkar's Communication Philosophy

Dr. B.R. Ambedkar enriched the Indian legacy through his historical contributions for educational, social, economic and political reformation of India before and after independence. Ambedkar strived all through his life for the empowerment of women and weaker sections against several odds. He was a multi-faceted great personality who has gone in history as a statesman whose contributions for the integrated development of the mankind regardless of religion, region, colour, caste, creed, etc. will be cherished for ever. He is also rightly remembered in the history of Indian media as the founder of 'parallel communication and journalism'. Unfortunately, the communities of knowledge and communities of power in India are united in their marginalization of Ambedkar who was a symbol of revolt against all oppressive features of Indian society.

The mass media in India have continued to ignore the socially and economically oppressed sections. The media in India are by and large, under the total monopoly of the ruling class which is the biggest enemy of the oppressed sections. The untold miseries of the weak and oppressed sections are not adequately focused by the Indian media. The contribution of the Indian mass media towards progressive social, economic, political and cultural movements is highly insignificant. It has been proved beyond all reasonable doubts that Indian media lack social commitment since it has always stood by the privileged sections of the Indian society. There are quite a few honourable exceptions in the history of Indian media who are wedded to social justice and empowerment of weaker sections of the society. Raja Ram Mohun Roy, Ranade, James Augustus Hickey, Gokhale, Azad, Phuley, Ambedkar, Periyar, Narayana Guru and Gundappa are the milestones of Indian media who were the voice of the voiceless.

Ambedkar was greatly influenced by the teachings of world's great Master Gautam Buddha. He was also considerably influenced by John Dewy, Booker T. Washington, J.S. Mill, Carlyl, Karl Marx, Kabir, Mahatma Phule and other rationalists. He was a rationalist to the core and did not believe in anything that appeared to him devoid of reason and morality. He accepted Lord Buddha's theory of the indomitable faith in the capacity of man to shape his own destiny and this theory and experience was a decisive factor which exercised a lasting influence on him. Ambedkar cultivated the rational spiritual perspective which influenced his writings, speeches and struggles. His communication philosophy was greatly influenced by these Eastern and Western philosophers who fought for collective welfare.

Ambedkar wanted the formal and informal educational institutions to provide life-oriented, mission-oriented, emancipation-oriented and empowerment-oriented education to the oppressed sections of Indian society. He firmly argued that the oppressed sections of India society would compete successfully with the upper classes if they are given better environment, resources, opportunities and facilities. In his writings Ambedkar emphasized that there is no genetic discrimination inflicted by Divinity on the SC/ST and other weaker sections of the society. It is society, the disabling environment, the penurious privations and the long distance from intellectual, industrial, educational and cultural opportunities and social suppressions for sinful centuries which have kept these millions of Indian humans in dark and depressed serfdom.

The main object of Ambedkar's life was to bring social revolution. He wanted to break the system of varnas and caste so that everybody gets the opportunity of self-development. For this he adopted a democratic and constitutional means. His communicative approaches were dominated by constitutional and democratic ideologies. He wanted to transform the political democracy into social democracy. Ambedkar accorded a place of pride to the freedom of speech and expression in the Constitution of India. He wanted the media institutions to function freely, fairly and fearlessly as the voice of the people in India. He rightly considered the media professionals as the representatives of the people and created equal opportunities for the media professionals and general publics with respect to freedom of speech and expression in the Constitution of India.

Ambedkar used his papers and other media effectively to expose the numerous Hindu myths, mysticisms and mumbo-jumbos justifying the injustices of Indian society. He broke the shackles of traditionalism, religious orthodoxy and blind superstitions. He bluntly rejected the whole system of Brahminical religion—the infallibility of the Vedas, transmigration of souls, the efficacy of rites and rituals, the '*moksha*' after the cycle of births, and '*Iswara*' as the creator of universe. He also rejected the whole of Upnishadic thought as mere imagination. He opposed out and out the '*Chaturvarnya*' system, which was made a 'sacred institution' and a 'divine ordination'. He concluded that there cannot be a more degrading system of social organization than '*Chaturvarnya*' which deadens, paralyses and cripples the people from helpful activities in Indian society.

Ambedkar firmly advocated 'Freedom of the Press'. He had a clear vision of the importance of the 'Press Freedom'. He accorded a pride of place to 'Freedom of Speech and Expression' which is the mother of all liberties while drafting the Constitution of India. One of the main objectives of the Constitution, as envisaged in the preamble, is to secure liberty of thought and expression to all the citizens. Ambedkar propagated his revolutionary ideas, views and experiences through his newspapers, namely—*Mookanayak* (Leader of the Dumb), *Bahiskrit Bharat* (Excluded India), *Samata* (Equality), *Janata* (People) and *Prabuddha Bharata* (Enlightened India).

Ambedkar's communication philosophy laid emphasis on the spread of knowledge and literacy in Indian society since he rightly thought that the non-Brahmins were denied the right to education, participation and progress in India. He strongly advocated in his writings that India must rise as a good State guaranteeing equal status in matters religious, social, economic and political, to all classes, offering every man an opportunity to rise in the scale of life and creating conditions favourable to his advancement.

Ambedkar advocated that the uplift of people in India should take place on the basis of equality and humanism. He had vehemently criticized the Brahmin monopoly over education, media and polity. His perception of humanism in the Indian context was par excellence. He rightly argued that individual should be the unit of national development and that caste based backwardness and exploitation should not continue in India. He waged a relentless war against the politics of oppression through his writings and speeches. He heralded a new era of social justice-oriented mass communication in India through Mookanayak. Ambedkar started a fortnightly Marathi paper, '*Bahiskrit Bharath*' on April 3, 1927 in Bombay in order to motivate the excluded sections of Indian society to actively participate in the mainstream of development. Dhananjay Keer (1954), a close associate of Ambedkar makes the following observation on the role played by Ambedkar as the editor of '*Bahiskrit Bharat*': "Ambedkar now began to explain his views, define his aims and reply to the critics of his movement through the new journal which is a milestone in Indian Journalism."

Ambedkar had to face floods of criticism from caste Hindu institutions and media which attributed motives to him. He bounced back and wrote: "The religion which discriminates between two followers is partial. The religion which treats crores of its adherents worse than dogs and criminals and inflicts upon them insufferable disabilities is no religion at all. Religion is not the appellation for such an unjust order. Religion and slavery are incompatible." Ambedkar used media for propagating revolutionary ideas and approaches which liberated the mankind from the exploitative tendencies carried out in the name of religion and god in India.

Ambedkar was highly critical about the media contents and skeptical about their outcome. He strongly argued for the abolition of caste system in India and emulated the thoughts and deeds of Buddha and Kabir in integrating the people of India since they were guided by reason and right kind of thinking about the betterment of the deprived sections of society. Ambedkar burnt '*Manusmriti*' on December 25, 1927 as a mark of social revolt against caste system and pleaded for the establishment of just society. Ambedkar actively participated in the Round Table Conferences as a true representative of the oppressed Indians. For the first time in the history of 2000 years, the voice of the depressed classes echoed in England. His followers expressed their gratitude by presenting with a purse which he used for stating another fortnightly named '*Janata*' (people).

In the struggle for the freedom of the country Gandhi had the support of the millions of Indians, but in the struggle for liberation of untouchables millions opposed him. Not even those for whom he struggled and bore patiently the humiliations and accusations hurled at him fully appreciated what he was doing, mainly because of the ignorance and lack of understanding, observe Bhagwan Das. Ambedkar wanted to secure social and economic independence to his people. Once he wrote: "Political power cannot be a panacea for the ills of the depressed classes. Their salvation lies in their social elevation. They must cleanse the evil habits. They must improve their bad ways of living. The movement will result in the emancipation of our people and the establishment of such a state of society in this country of ours in which one man will have one value in all domains of life, political, social and economic."

His lieutenants Deorao Naik and Kadrekar started a new fortnightly paper called the *Janata*—the people. There was indeed, a strong and notable evolution of Ambedkar's role in the social, political and journalistic spheres of India. *Samata* (The Equality) and *Janata* (The People) were the third and fourth papers edited by Ambedkar. "The leader of the dumb made a stir and described the sufferings of the outcastes in the first stage. He wrote plenty of things and condemned the persecution of depressed classes in the second stage. He gave expression to their aspirations for equality in the third stage. He expressed the desire of his people for assimilation into Hindu society on the basis of equality, liberty and fraternity in the fourth stage."

Ambedkar was not able to sustain the journals mainly due to economic constraint. He could not bring out his papers regularly because many people including his own followers did not read them mainly due to immaturity and helplessness. Ambedkar brought out the journals as the mouth piece of all oppressed sections of Indian society. That apart, Ambedkar was not prepared to compromise with the professional ethics. He did not become an agent of the capitalists like most of the editors of his time. He never had any inclination towards commercialization of his papers.

Ambedkar consciously supported the British during the World War II since he was a born democrat. Many people and papers called him as the stooge of British. Ambedkar considered that it was a war between dictatorship and democracy. Nazism was the menace to the future of mankind, and so it was the duty of every lover of democracy to see that dictatorship vanishes and democracy grows. If democracy dies, he observed, 'it will be their doom'. Ambedkar firmly believed in democracy as a means of self-respect, equality and growth. He called upon the media to assume the role of watch dogs of public interest in a democratic society.

Ambedkar's writings duly emphasized the importance of education, agitation and organization which were the principal tools of social justice, economic uplift and political democracy for the oppressed classes in India. He ridiculed the Congress Press which constantly indulged in criticizing, rebuking and reviling Ambedkar for everything. He observed: "Nothing I do, pleases the Congress Press. This animosity of the Congress Press towards me can to my mind not unfairly, be explained as a reflex of the hatred of the Hindus for the untouchables. That their animosity has become personal is clear from the fact that the Congress Press feels offended for my having criticized Mr. Jinnah who has been the butt and the target of the Congress for the last several years. However, strong and however filthy be the abuse which the Congress Press chooses to shower on me I must do my duty. I am not worshipper of idols. I believe in breaking them. I insist that if I hate Mr. Gandhi and Mr. Jinnah—I dislike them. I do not hate them—it is because I love India more. That is the true faith of a nationalist. I have hopes that my countrymen, will someday learn that the country is greater than the men, that the worship of Mr. Gandhi or Mr. Jinnah and service to India are two very different things and may even be contradictory of each other." Ambedkar's approach to issues relating to Indian media is not merely reflected in the provisions of the Indian Constitution, relating to social responsibility of media but also in the views that he expressed in various fora.

Ambedkar's quest for social justice through constitutional safeguards and media services remain as the milestone of Indian media system. He was the most articulate spokesman of the exploited and downtrodden in Indian society and media. He constantly reminded the government, media and society of their responsibilities towards the depressed classes through his forceful speeches and writings. Ambedkar's philosophy of communication and journalism revolved around social justice and empowerment through constitutional and democratic means. Ambedkar rightly emphasized that the lofty ideals expressed in the Constitution would remain as they were, given the nature of contradictions inherent in Indian society, polity, media, economy and so on. He called upon the media institutions to strive for the attainment of social and economic equality. He also cautioned the rulers to wipe out social and economic inequality which would eventually blow up the structure of political democracy which was laboriously built up by the Constituent Assembly.

Ambedkar constantly upheld Buddhist way of life which was based on fraternity, equality, liberty and collective welfare. He strongly opposed Marx's method which brought about equality at the cost of fraternity and freedom. According to him, Buddhist system was a democratic system where as the communist system was based on dictatorship. His spirituality was based on the Buddhist principle of non-violence. Ambedkar was a great communicator with a difference. His observation on Indian press provides a glimpse of his perception and practice which are upheld with great reverence by those who consider media as the instruments of human progress.

It reads : "Journalism in India was once a profession. It has now become a trade. It has no more moral function than the manufacture of soap. It does not regard itself as the responsible adviser of the public. To give the news uncolored by any motive, to present a certain view of public policy which it believes to be for the good of the community, to correct and chastise without fear all those, no matter how high, who have chosen a wrong or a barren path, is not regarded by journalism in India its first or foremost duty. To accept a hero and worship him has become its principal duty. Under it, news gives place to sensation, reasoned opinion to under reasoning passion, appeal to the minds of responsible people to appeal to the emotions of the irresponsible. Salisbury spoke of the Northcliffe journalism as written by office-boys for office-boys. Indian journalism is all that plus something more. It is written by drum boys to glorify their heroes. Never the hero worship became so blind that as we see it in India today. There are, I am glad to say, honorable exceptions. But they are too few and their voice is never heard. Entrenched behind the plaudits of the Press, the spirit of domination exhibited by these two great men has transgressed all limits. By their domination they have made half their followers fools and the other half hypocrites. In establishing their supremacy they have taken the aid of 'big business' and money magnates. For the first time in our country money is taking the field as organized power. The questions which President Roosevelt propounded for American public to consider will arise here, if they have not already arisen: Who shall rule—wealth or man? Which shall lead—money or intellect? Who shall fill public stations, educated and patriotic free men or the feudal serfs of corporate capital?" Ambedkar had critically analysed the role of capitalists in modern jounralism with due respect to social justice.

Ambedkar dedicated his life to the cause of millions of oppressed Indians including untouchables. He breathed his last on December 6, 1956. The nation mourned the death of Ambedkar who had played a historical role for over four decades as the emancipator of oppressed class and champion of the have-nots in Indian society. Ambedkar utilized the newspapers as channels of progressive communication which intended to create a just society in India. He also addressed millions of people through radio and enlightened them through his thought provoking speeches. He utilized public meetings and group discussions as prominent channels of communication. He published several books which provide better food for thought and action. He accorded great importance to mass communication with a view to propagate his revolutionary ideas and justify his actions inside and outside the Parliament.

While most of the communicators of his times did their best to champion the cause of the haves, Ambedkar putforth his best efforts to champion the cause of the have nots. His innings as a mass communicator was superb. His writings and speeches were based on systematic research and evaluation. Even his critics were impressed by his thought provoking communication in various media. The greatest contribution of Ambedkar to Indian media was his attempt to create a parallel media in Indian society on the basis of standardized and humanitarian principles and practices of mass communication and journalism. The basic message of his works is that control of minds by some powerful individuals, press and other media is bad as such control retards movement. He felt that mind control by mass media and drug is the awesome reality. Ambedkar had rightly cautioned that media owned by the capitalist and casteist forces should not pollute the minds of the people.

Ambedkar argued that commercialization of media is highly detrimental from the point of view of establishing an egalitarian society. He suggested that the remedy lies in making knowledge free and in widening the frontiers of practical social wisdom. It is in this context that the rationalism of Ambedkar is revealed to all of us who prize the liberty to know, to utter and to argue freely according to conscience, above all liberties. He advocated that mass media should not be allowed to become the handmade of the corrupt and dominant section of the society. Ambedkar occupies a position of high eminence among the communicators, scholars and statesmen for his revolutionary thoughts, deeds and contributions. His name will remain ever green in the history of mankind as a symbol of revolt and champion of the downtrodden communities.

Indian Communication Policy Formulation and Mission

India is the land of global visionaries, missionaries and statesmen who excelled as great communicators. Buddha laid a strong foundation for the Indian communication policy-making 2500 years ago. Several scholars have explored the wide spectrum of teachings and cultural forms that come under the name of Buddhism. Communication enjoys a place of pride only in a democratic system. The Indian communication policy was formulated by Buddha informally since he firmly believed that democracy should be basically built on the idea of freedom of the mind of the people who matter most. The ideals of democracy and freedom of the mind are woven into the very structure of Buddhism. Buddha established the world's first democracy in India and emphatically taught the principles of liberty, equality, fraternity and justice. Buddha advocated that a true democracy is the system of governance by the people and allows free speech based on rationality.

In India 'Panchayats' were established 2500 years ago under the influence of Buddhism. In Asia, there were great civilizations but not great democracies like India. Mahathera Piyadassi (1991) writes: "The similarity between Buddhism and democracy is perceived in the teachings of the Buddha. His advocation of tolerance, the idea of discussion, extraordinary freedom of choice, equality, non-violence, impermanence—everyone of these ideas went against the customs of his times. They were revolutionary concepts introduced by the Buddha 2500 years ago. They were major intellectual innovations. But they were all democratic in content and intent." Buddha also produced outstanding kings, namely Ashoka the great in the third century B.C., Kanishka in the second century B.C., Harsha in the eighth century A.C. and others who made India a super power and a model state much before the industrial revolution in the West. These Buddhist rulers understood and implemented the communication policy of Buddha and contributed historically towards making India the world's foremost democracy and welfare state.

King Ashoka is regarded as one of the most just, wise and benevolent rulers of all time in India. He considered all the citizens as his own children and wanted them to enjoy all property and happiness on par with the king. He had rightly perceived that there is no duty higher than to promote the happiness of the whole world. H.G. Wells (1934) writes: "Amidst the tens of thousands of monarchs.....that crowd the columns of history the name of Ashoka shines and shines almost alone, a star."

Jawaharlal Nehru, the first Prime Minister of India, addressing the members of the Indian National Congress remarked: "I have enough faith in me to bow my head when the Buddha's name is mentioned. The path which the Buddha and Ashoka had shown has not been forgotton and has somehow remained in the minds of India. Mahatma Gandhi followed the same path in our lifetime and following that path the prestige and strength of the nation was raised. If any question has to be considered it has to be considered peacefully and democratically in the way taught by the Buddha."

The great foundation thinkers of the Western world Socrates, Plato and Aristotle rejected democracy as an unsuitable form of government. In the 12th century, Basava established '*Anubhava Mantapa*' in Karnataka and facilitated social, economic, political and cultural justice to the people regardless of religion, region, gender and so on. Basava established a casteless society in Karnataka and made Karnataka a model state politically and otherwise. Basava also groomed many progressive thinkers and writers who produced radical literature which stood by the principle of collective welfare. Basava also gave a radical dimension to the communication philosophy in India.

In Western Europe, rational democratic movement was built under the leadership of John Milton during 18th century. The Western thinkers strongly advocated that priests and kings should not boss over the people who were born with the fundamental right to self-governance and development. The principle of liberal democracy which inspired the founders of American Constitution was that controversial questions should be decided by argument rather than by force. The first amendment to the Constitution of America clearly stated that Congress shall make no law abridging the freedom of press.

Democracy depends on active public instruction, discussion and participation. The democracy is also based on the consent of the people who are the makers of their own destinies. The government has the responsibility to encourage innovative communication initiatives in order to facilitate meaningful nation building on the basis of active and intelligent democratic participation. Statesmen across the world have emphasized the need to device strategies and build channels of communication that operate both upwards and downwards and laterally so as to generate wider participation of people in the process of nation building.

Joseph Pulitzer who is known in the world as the founding father of value based journalism advocated the communication policy which promoted professional ethics and safeguarded public interest long ago. The *North American Review* has quoted the observation made by Pulitzer with respect to media policy in a democratic set-up. It reads: "Our Republic and its press will rise or fall together. A cynical, mercenary, demagogic press will produce in time a people as base as itself." Pulitzer firmly believed that journalism is more than just a way to make money or provide entertainment. He also advocated that journalism serve the people and uphold professional values as a fourth estate. Thus, Pulitzer provided a sound ideological framework for the formulation of communication policy in the world.

The Indian national leaders were greatly influenced by the European and American liberal political philosophy. Ambedkar, the chief architect of the Indian Constitution was greatly inspired by Buddhist ideology and Western liberalism. He incorporated the fundamental rights and duties of the people in the Constitution which precisely demonstrate the Indian communication policy. Ambedkar incorporated the Buddhist thoughts in the Constitution of India and created the Article 19(1)(a) which guarantees the freedom of speech and expression to all the citizens of India. Ambedkar strongly believed that in a democratic atmosphere, masters and slaves cannot exist together. He also advocated that democracy is individual salvation as well as national salvation.

The formulation of National Communication policy in India is influenced by the constitutional provisions and universal declaration on human rights. Article 19 to the Declaration of Human Rights (1948) states: "Everyone has the right to freedom of opinion and expression; the right includes freedom to hold opinions without interference and is to seek and receive and impart information and ideas through any media and regardless of frontiers." A similar declaration of the universal right to freedom of expression is embodied in Article 10 of the Resolution passed by the Council of Europe on November 4, 1950.

In post-Second World War era, India was the first country which, in tune with the United Nation's Declaration embodied in Article 19(1)(a) of the Constitution (1950), the 'guarantee of freedom of speech and expression' as a fundamental right, which, according to pronouncements of the Supreme Court, includes the 'freedom of the press and right to information'. The Constitution of India is committed to giving every individual his/her right place and raises each one from lower to higher levels. Ambedkar also incorporated series of reasonable restrictions to the Constitution of India with respect to freedom of expression under Article 19-b. The fundamental rights in general and freedom of speech and expression in particular precisely deal with the Indian communication policy in the post-independence era. "The formulation of a communication policy needs to be undertaken by the policy makers on the assumption that freedom of information and right to information are essential components of participatory democracy", writes Manonmani (1997).

Mahatma Gandhi was the great visionary of the 20th century. He was inspired by the history of India and strongly pleaded for the collective welfare of all Indians in the post-independence era. His communication and development philosophies absolutely reflected the Buddhist aspirations as rightly stated by Jawaharlal Nehru. Gandhi wanted to establish '*Ram Raj*' in India which paved the way for free discussion, democratic participation and humanitarian progress of the mankind in India regardless of caste, color, creed and so on. He was killed by the fundamentalists of Hindu society who were opposed to collective welfare and communal harmony in the post-independence era. Gandhi also gave an ideological foundation for the Indian communication policy in his writings and speeches. The Gandhian communication policy conveyed the principles of non-violence and democratic agitation which became the powerful tools for mass communication in India.

Ram Manohar Lohia was a great socialist who also fought for social and economic justice within and outside the Parliament. He had dreamt of creating an egalitarian society in India through adoption of secularism, socialism, humanism and other democratic principles. Lohia had rightly called upon the backwards, *dalits* and minorities to get united under the leadership of Ambedkar and establish a welfare state in the post-independence era. He also firmly believed in the freedom of speech and expression and argued strongly for the development of media systems as the voice of the people and tools of development of the country. The Indian communication policy also represents the socialistic and democratic aspirations of Lohia.

Jaya Prakash Narayan was a great national leader who led socialist and democratic movement in India after Nehru. He should have been the natural choice for the post of Prime Minister after the death of Nehru. He was not prepared to compromise with the values he firmly believed for the sake of power politics. He also advocated that media in India should function in accordance with the Constitutional obligations and human values. He led the total revolution movement during 1975-77 when Indira Gandhi had imposed national emergency in India against the Constitutional provisions. He also built a strong national movement for the restoration of democracy and freedom of speech and expression in India. He succeeded in the downfall of Congress government and successfully installed the first non-Congress government headed by Morarji Desai. His writings and speeches adequately demonstrate the liberal and democratic aspirations which have inspired the national leaders to grant autonomy to electronic media in India. Jaya Prakash Narayan was a great champion of democracy, social justice and responsible media in India.

The need for a national communication policy is widely debated in India. Subhas Chandra Bose had set up a National Planning

Committee in 1938 under the Chairmanship of Jawaharlal Nehru to study the role of media in national development. He wanted the mass media to facilitate the development of the nation by creating informed and active citizens. Since then, several committees and commissions are set up to examine the management and functions of mass media and formulate meaningful communication policy in the country. Prominent among them include—Chanda Committee, Verghese Committee, Joshi Committee, Paswan Committee, Pawar Committee and so on. Several national seminars are also organized to deliberate upon the issues, challenges and responsibilities concerning the formulation of national communication policy in India. However, there is no comprehensive national communication policy formulation till now in India.

Kiran Karnik (1995) observes: "Before the discussion about policy it needs to understand the media environment, the new technological developments that have already taken place and those that are emerging and also the nature of the particular society. In the absence of such familiarity, any policy framework is likely to be meaningless and divorced from reality."

Dangwal (2000) underlines the significance of a viable national communication policy in the age of globalization thus: "The trend towards national and international monopoly over the media has posed and is posing a grave threat to the survival of democracy itself. With monopoly over the news and views, the media barons are in a position to suppress, manipulate and distort information. The monopoly over news and views, whether of the government or private individuals, is detrimental to democracy. In such circumstances, the freedom of press as is generally spoken or understood is far away from the reality."

Ravishankar Prasad (2002) observed that the fast emerging situation in the age of globalization has posed certain very important questions like creation of monopolies, cross-media restrictions and survival of small and medium newspapers. He agreed that the Government of India has to play a major role in safeguarding the public interest against the media abuse and manipulation. The government is called upon to assume the regulatory role in view of the proliferation of channels. The multiplication of media and proliferation of channels have necessitated the need of an independent regulator for broadcasting sector in the country.

Scholars have prevailed upon the government to protect the interest of the people by juxtaposing the self-regulation with the overpowering commercialization in order to humanize the face of globalization. The government has to come out with a national communication policy on the basis of wide-ranging consultations with the media stakeholders. The fast changing technology had completely changed the media environment, but any delay in embracing these changes would be disastrous to the Indian Republic under the changed circumstances.

That there is no philosophy of communication underpinning the management and functions of the Indian media. Nandini Sahai (2002) comments: "The exclusion of the poor from communication resources is part of a vicious circle in which socio-economic backwardness goes hand in hand with deprivation and exclusion. The mainstream media, whether state-owned or private has subordinated itself to the ruling elite, and by and large reflects its priorities and values, in its of coverage of news and its programming contents, rather than the interest of the poor, which often conflict with those of the elite."

In India, the mass media are required to conform to well established theories of communication such as social responsibility active people's participation and development orientation which should be in conformity with the constitutional guarantee of freedom of speech and expression. The government is free to frame certain guidelines and supervise the media activities thus screening out objectionable, sensational, seditious, contemptuous and unhealthy materials. According to Justice P.B. Savant, former Chairman of Press Council of India, the freedom of the media is essentially the freedom of the society to be informed accurately and adequately on all matters which affect public interest. Gupta (1994) had undertaken an extensive review of communication policies in India at various stages in the post-independence era and suggested that the Central Government should formulate national communication policy in view of the convergence of various information and communication technologies which have opened up a plethora of new possibilities and threats in India in view of globalization.

The laws relating to media, human rights and development are framed in India from time to time in accordance with the Constitutional norms and guidelines. The communication policy is a very important subject dealing with several essential aspects relating to Indian media management. However, there is growing concern in the country about issues relating to communication policy formulation in India. The successive governments have consciously reviewed the existing media laws, procedures and system of management of media with a view to bring about greater media accountability and devise efficient and effective methods of dealing with various situations concerning good governance and responsible media management in the changing social, political and economic circumstances.

The Supreme Court and Parliament have been watching the functions of various communications media in India especially in the age of globalization. Strong arguments are placed by various progressive individuals and organizations to constitute national media commission and national media council in order to enforce disciplinary mechanisms and socially responsible media services in India. The Indian Penal Code also contains several norms and guidelines with respect to protection of public interest against defamatory, irresponsible, seditious and unethical media services.

The successive Governments in India have recognized the need and importance of the free media, independent media, responsible media and responsive media in India in the post-independence era. The national leaders have upheld the Constitutional provisions for a free and responsible media system and operations in India. The Indian media laws are also enacted with due respect to the Constitutional aspirations and teachings of national leaders who stood by socialist and democratic principles of media management and national governance. The governments have not formulated a formal communication policy in India even after 67 years of national independence. But the communications media in India are regulated as per the Constitutional norms and philosophies of Buddha, Ashoka, Basava, Gandhi, Nehru, Ambedkar, Lohia, Jaya Prakash Narayan and other statesmen, nation builders and scholars.

Several regional and national seminars are also organized since independence in order to facilitate better communication policy-making in India. Various communication scholars, scientists, professionals, activists and others have also placed their opinions in their writings and speeches with regard to the formulation of national communication policy in India. Several communication theologizers have also provided certain theological perspectives on communication policy formulation with reference to India. In the age of globalization, we find that the whole rhythm of change in the field of communication has such a momentum that government is far behind compared to the media corporate houses as a whole.

The government should consider the fact that media institutions are intimately connected to the society and pay attention to communication policy formulation at the national level. In other words, an awareness of the importance of communication policy in India is not lacking at the theoretical or practical level of media management. However, there is hardly any successful attempt at political level in integrating communication within the overall context of inclusive development of people in Indian Republic. A coherent national communication policy is essential in India at this juncture in order to facilitate the inclusive and integrated development of the marginalized sections of the Indian society.

The communication experts and philosophers have observed that a national communication policy is the key to manage the Indian media in right direction and spirit. Besides this, communication policy education has not occupied an important place in the national developmental agenda. In reality, a well defined and comprehensive national communication policy is practically non-existent in India despite several demands. Various committees and individuals have highlighted the need for the formulation of national communication policy in the age of globalization in order to exercise suitable checks and balances against the irresponsible functioning of various media institutions which have accorded priority for commercialization of communication services at the social and developmental costs over a period of time. The policy makers are required to collect, consolidate and correlate appropriate ideas and strategies in order to formulate a viable national communication policy in the new millennium.

The Future of Indian Communication Media

The growing media monopoly and the consequent alienation from the constitutional obligations have serious implications for the future of the media institutions in India. The critics of globalization have given a serious thought to the formulation of national communication policy in India in order to safeguard the public interest in accordance with the ethical norms, professional obligations and constitutional provisions.

Somnath Chatterji (2007) former Speaker of Lok Sabha lamented that the hey days of great editors who virtually set the standards of impartiality and independence that became an integral part of the print media are not to be found anymore. But unfortunately other factors came into play. Chief among them was the advent of technology that made it possible to print millions of copies and set pages of computer, making production not only fast but more economical. Then the satellite age made it possible to send content from one office to another so that local editions could be produced simultaneously. Another factor was the burgeoning advertising industry and the enormous amounts of money it poured into the newspaper and journals. Indeed, it is said that today some newspapers can afford to give away their copies for free since their revenue, that may run to crores of rupees. Chatterji had called upon the owners and professionals to function responsibly in Indian democracy.

In the present times, more importance is now given to the marketing division of a newspaper rather than editorial department. The marketing department has gained an upper hand over the editorial department because salability of news matters most than the quality of the news. The national news is relegated to the inside pages because of the influence of FDI and globalization of media. *The Hindu* (2007) has pointed out that this tendency of the newspaper is the direct impact of liberalism and consumerism.

The news relating to poverty, hunger, ill health, malnutrition, famine, unemployment etc. that affect the lives of the millions of people in India are trivialized. The urban and rural divide and rich and poor divide are increasing in the age of globalization. The print media have a social obligation in the country and function as effective watch dogs of public interest. The press and the government are required to function in a climate of understanding and partnership in order to protect the national interest and facilitate the inclusive development of the disadvantaged sections of the society in future.

The Indian film market has been expanded and Indian Diaspora is taking active part in both film production and film viewing. India is producing the largest number of news reels, documentaries and feature films in the world. Most of the feature films are produced on the basis of box office economics with a view to earn money at the cost of professional excellence and artistic norms. The Government of India have declared film making as an industry and the banks and other financial institutions have come forward to provide financial assistance to the film makers. The National Film Development Corporation has also provided subsidized financial assistance for the production of quality-oriented new wave films in the country. The Indian film industry needs to be disciplined through proper norms and guidelines in order to safeguard public interest. The Indian film industry has to rise to the occasion in meeting the demands of the people and fulfilling the constitutional obligations.

The electronic media have grown considerably on account of liberalization of electronic media and granting of autonomy. The satellite channels have continued to create local consumers for the products of multi national corporations. The radio continues to be a decent medium of communication. But the language, contents and focus of FM stations are not up to the mark professionally. The private television channels are known for broadcasting maximum entertainment and advertisement programmes which have not contributed to the healthy growth of the language, culture, human values and mankind in India.

Media critic Sham Lal (2003) cautions: "Whatever, the media gurus might say the truth is that a visual culture, for all the extravagant hopes invested in it will remain a matter of service. The idea of death is strange to it. How can it be otherwise when it is run by market forces and rigged competition permits new hegemonies not only in the field of new industries but also in the media in any case unjust to blame the media alone for trivialization. The business of commodifying these is a collective enterprise in which the main actor on the political stage play a more decisive role and those who merely report or comment on what goes on in places where big decisions are made. In tele democracy many speak. In the first many are lost in one; in the second one is lost in many. In a pathological, pluralistic society like India, a government can find loose its way assigned as it has all the time to buy many discontent voices each imploring to go in different directions. The media does its bit in adding to the mayhem. Looking at the way the television is conducting itself is clear that all the evils of globalization is being manifested through various television programmes."

Arvind Rajgopal (2001) notes: "The television is affecting the native language, tradition and culture. It has been shamelessly used by politicians to push their ideology. The television is also altering the ideology of masses and is misused by Hindu fundamentalists. Two mega serials—*Ramayana* and *Mahabharata* on television altered the political course of the country. Unfortunately, the regulations we have made to control the contents of television is totally inadequate."

The *Asian Age* (2001) identifies the lapse of the government with respect to regulating the contents of private television channels. It reads: "The government may not have succeeded in publishing through a content code to regulate the country's private television channels. Nevertheless, it does hope to tighten the screws on private channels where their content is concerned in the wake of what it says are increasing complaints regarding 'undesirable content' and 'malpractices by cable operators'."

The mainstream electronic media have failed to check the menace of globalization in India. The electronic media have resorted to mind pollution, guerilla advertising and other unethical practices which have harmed the public interest in India. The tendency of cross ownership has brought about the decline of the standard of broadcasting in India. However, All India Radio and Doordarshan have not compromised with professional and constitutional obligations and standards. They are facing the worst possible competition from the private channels which have taken the professional values and audience for granted. Hence, the functioning of electronic media including the private channels need to be disciplined and standardized in India through proper broadcasting policy initiatives and controlling mechanisms.

The new communication technologies have become prominent instruments of globalization of knowledge. India has become a prominent new media power thanks to the innovative measures launched by the policy makers in the age of globalization. Technological changes have transformed the speed, capacity and sophistication of telecommunication, satellite and computer systems. The digitalization of television, telephone, computer and other services has been accompanied a variety of alliances and projects. The digital divide continues to remain in India in the new millennium. The policy makers are required to formulate new media policy with a view to expedite the processes of decentralization, democratization, localization and humanization of new media. The intelligent and active application of social media for various developmental endeavours should be spelt out in the new media policy of the government.

The mainstream media in India (both traditional and modern) have failed to translate the constitutional obligations into realities in the post-independence era. The communications media in India continue to remain as the class media rather than mass media. The media have grown enormously in India but today the demassification of media demassifise our minds as well according to Toffler (1992). Despite demassification of media, new media initiatives are cropping up in India and abroad in order to contain the growth of new imperialist forces and facilitate interactive communication, development communication, human rights communication and judicious communication in India. The government should formulate a national communication policy which would strengthen the new initiatives for alternative media in the country. It would also safeguard the interest of the majority of the people who are isolated, marginalized and disadvantaged due to several constraints and compulsions.

Epilogue

The globalization has impacted the media services in India and abroad. There are advantages and disadvantages of globalization with reference to media management in the present times. But the disadvantages outweigh the advantages according to the ground realities which are reflected adequately in the empirical studies. The present work emphasizes that it is imperative to formulate a national policy on communication at this juncture of entry of foreign media, invasion of satellite channels, prevailing pluralistic media culture, centralized media services and commercialized media scenario in India. This has been a long pending demand for the formulation of an ideal national media policy in India. The Government of India may consider constituting an expert committee of legal luminaries, media experts, media scholars, social activists and intellectuals for evolving an authentic, comprehensive and purposeful national communication policy at this juncture.

The Government of India may also consider constituting a National Media Commission consisting of scholars and activists drawn from different spheres of human life to monitor the media scenario in the country in the age of globalization and make the media institutions accountable to the Parliament and people. The National Commission may also advice the Government of India and other agencies regarding the expansion, decentralization, democratization and humanization of communication services in the country. It is high time the Press Council of India is converted into Media Council of India in order to regulate the functions of both traditional and modern communications media and uphold professional ethics. India needs a communication strategy which should be considered as a sub-system of development process at national, regional and community levels.

The observation made by Aravind Sinha (2006) aptly reveals the significance of national communication policy in India. It reads: "Since the expansion and reach of interest has multiplied after the Third Wave was published, the demassification of the media is surging ahead at a faster phase in the age of globalization. A whole set of new nation channels has sprung up to confront the mainstream media and to oppose globalization and war. The peace movement, the anti-WTO movement and the World Social Forum is capable of opposing global powers without the support of mainstream media and with the help of the Internet and other modes of communication. This is how an alternative media is developing in the world. Along with the struggle of human race for democracy, freedom, dignity and equity, this alternative media will continue to grow and develop as a simultaneous process."

Bibliography

Aggrawal, Vir Bala and V.S. Gupta (2001). *Handbook of Journalism and Mass Communication*, New Delhi: Concept Publishing Company.

Amin, Samir (2004). *The Liberal Virus: Permanent War and the Americanization of the World*. London: Pluto Press.

Anderson, B. (1991). *Imagined Communities: Reflections on the Origin and Spread of Nationalism*. London: Verso.

Anthropological Survey of India (1998). *Survey on Impact of Globalisation on Indian Culture*, New Delhi, India.

Argenti, P.A. (1996). Corporate communication as a discipline: toward a definition, *Management Communication Quarterly*, 10(1): 73–97.

Argentini, Paul A. (1998). *Corporate Communication*, Boston: Irwin/ McGraw-Hill, p.167.

Arnander, Christopher (2004). *Think Globally, Spend Locally*, London : Profile Books.

Banerjee, I. (2002). The Locals Strike Back? Media Globalization and Localization in the New Asian Television Landscape. Gazette: *The International Journal for Communication Studies,* 64(6), 517-535.

Barnet, R.J. and Cavanagh, J. (1994). *Global Dreams: Imperial Corporations and the New World Order*, Simon and Schuster.

Barnouw, Erik and Krishnaswamy, S. (1980). *Indian Film,* New Delhi : Oxford University Press.

Baskin, Otis, Craig Aronoff and Dan Lattimore (1997). *Preface to Public Relations: The Profession and the Practice*, Madison : Brown and Benchmark Publishers, p. xiii.

Belch, George E. and Michael E. Belch (2003). *Advertising and Promotion: An Integrated Marketing Communications Perspective*, New Delhi : TMH.

Beltran, Luis Ramiro (1978). Rural Communities in Developing Countries:

The Prospects of Communication, *Issues in Communication*. No. 2, International Institute of Communications, London, UK.

Benzason and Sagasti (1995). The Elusive Search: Development and Progress in the Transition to a New Century, Ottowa : International Development Research Center.

Berle, A. and Means, G. (1932). *The Modern Corporation and Private Property.* Harcourt, New York : Brace and World.

Berlo, David K. (1978). *The Process of Communication*, New York : Sage Publications.

Bhatia, Sapna (2002). Media Culture, Marketisation and Globalisation, *Communication Today*, 5(4):17-27.

Bloch, L.R. and Lemish, D. (2003). The Megaphone Effect: The International Diffusion of Cultural Media Via The USA, in P.J. Kalbfleisch (Ed.), *Communication Year Book*, 27:159-190.

Boro, Anil (2006). Globalizaton and Local Cultures:The Tribes of North East India, *Indian Folklife,* Serial No. 22, July.

Boyd-Barrett, O. (1977). Media Imperialism: Towards An International Framework for the Analysis of Media Systems, in J.Curran and M.Gurevitch (eds). *Mass Communication and Society*, London: Edward Arnold, 116-135.

Cavanagh, J. and Mader, J. (2002). Alternatives to Economic Globalization:A Better World is Possible—A Report of the International Forum on Globalization, San Francisco: Berrett-Koehler Publishers, Inc, p.19.

Chauhan, N.B. (2004). Corrective Approaches of Communication for Sustainable Extension Services in India: National Workshop on Communication Support for Sustaining Extension Services, Department of Extension Education, Institute of Agricultural Sciences, Banaras Hindu University, Varanasi.

Chiovoloni, M. (2004). The Interactive Power of Local and Traditional Communication Systems, *Ileia Magazine*, April 28, pp. 1-4.

Chomsky, Noam (1989). *Necessary Illusions*, London : Pluto Press, p. 5.

Cohen, H. (2006). *Good Arabs: The Israeli Security Services and Israeli Arabs*. Jerusalem: Hebrew Publishing House.

Cutlip, Scott M., Allen H. Center and Glen M. Broom (2004). *Effective Public Relations*, Singapore : Pearson Education Private Limited, p. 6.

Dangwal, A.R. (2000). Freedom of Press in India: A Reality, *Third Concept*, 14(159-160): 73-78.

Davis, Keith (1977). *The Organizational Communicator*, New York : Harper and Row Publishers.

DeFleur, Melvin (1970). *Theories of Mass Communication*, New York : David McKay, p. 76.

Dennis, Everette (1992). *Of Media and People*, Newbury Park, Calif: Sage Publications.

Dias, Marco *et al.* (1979). *National Communication Policy Councils*, Paris: UNESCO.

Diock and Dimock (1936). *Public Administration*, New York : Rinehard and Co.

Dominick, Joseph (2002). *Many-to-Many Communication in the Age of Globalisation*, p. 23.

Dominick, Josheph, Barry Shermany and Gary Copeland (1996). *Broadcasting/Cable and Beyond*, New York: McGraw-Hill.

Downs, Cal W., Berg, David M. and Linkugel, Wil A. (1997). *The Organizational Communator*, New York : Harper and Row Publishers, p. 41.

Etzioni, Amitai (1993). *The Spirit of Community: Rights, Responsibilities, and the Communitarian Agenda*. New York: Crown Publishers.

Fischer, Desmond (1982). *The Right to Communicate*, Paris : UNESCO.

Fombrun, C. and Van Riel, C.B.M. (2004). *Fame and Fortune: How Successful Companies Build Winning Reputations*. London: FT Prentice Hall.

Ganley, Gladys D. (1992). *The Exploding Political Power of Personal Media*, Norwood, NJ: Ablex.

Gerbner, George (1985). Mass Media Discourse: Message System Analysis as a Component of Cultural Indicators, In T.A. Van Dijk (Ed). *Discourse and Mass Communication: New Approaches to the Analysis of Mass Media Discourse and Communication*, Berlin : Walterde Gruyter and Co., p. 76.

Giddens, A. (1999). *The Constitution of Society: Outline of the Theory of Structuration*, University of California Press: pp. 15-16.

Giroux, Henry A. (2009). Foreword, The Spectacle of Accumulation, Sutjhally (Ed.) Advertising at the Edge of the Apocalypse, *www.sutjhally.com*

Glenny, Misha (2008). *McMafia:A Journey Through the Global Criminal Underworld*. Bodley Head/New York: Alfred A. Knopf.

Gray, John (2003). *Al Qaeda and What It Means to Be Modern*, New York: Faber and Faber.

Grieco, M. and Holmes, L. (1999). Tele Options for Community Business: an opportunity for economic growth in Africa, *Africa Notes*, pp. 1-3.

Griffin, N. and Masters, K. (1997). *Hit and Run: How Jon Peters and Peter Guber took Sony for a ride in Hollywood*, New York: Touchstone Books.

Gupta, V.S. (1994). *Communication Policies: An Overview, Third Revolution in Indian Perspectives*, New Delhi: Anmol Publishers.

Hall, Dunn S.W. and A. Barban (1987). *Advertising, It's Role in Modern Marketing Advertising, Its Role in Modern Marketing*. Hindsdale, Illinois: Dryden Press.

Herman, Edward S. and Robert W. McChesney (1998). *The Global Media: The Missionaries of Corporate Capitalism*, New Delhi : Madhyam Books.

Hilger, Susanne (2008). Globalization by Americanization: American Companies and the Internationalization of German Industry after the Second World War, *European Review of History/Revue Europeenne d'Histoire*, 15(4) : 375–401.

Huntington, Samuel (1993). The Clash of Civilizations, *Foreign Affairs*, Summer.

Jeffrey, Robin (2000). *India's Newspaper Revolution, Capitalism, Politics and Indian Language Press: 1977 to 1999*, New Delhi: Oxford University Press, p. 72.

Jhully, Sut (2009). Advertising at the Edge of the Apocalypse, www.sutjhally.com

Kamala, R. (2004). Forging a Link Between Indegenous Communication, Effective Community Social Work Practice and National Development, *Studies on Tribes Tribals*, 2(2): 89-95.

Kamlongera, C. (2000). Folk Media in Communication: For Development, A note. In: P. Van Der Stichele (Ed.) *Folk and Traditional Media for Rural Development, A workshop held in Malawis Liiongwe*, 23 August–3 September 1999, www.yahoo mail.com.

Karnik, Kiran (1995). National Policy for TV and Satellite Communication, Paper Presented in the National Colloquium on Media Policy, Indian Institute of Mass Communication, New Delhi, India.

Kaul, Asha (2002). *Business Communication*, New Delhi : Prentice Hall of India Private Limited, pp. 1-11.

Keer, Dhananjay (1954). *Dr. Ambedkar: Life and Mission*, Bombay : Popular Prakashan.

Khandekar, Vanita Kohli (2006). *Indian Media Business*, New Delhi : Concept Publishing Company.

Kissinger, Henry (1999). Special lecture delivered at the Trinity College, Dublin, October 12.

Klein, Naomi (2002). *Fences and Windows*, New Delhi : Leftword.

Kumar, Keval J. (2007). *Mass Communication in India*, Bombay: Jaico Paperbacks, Revised Ed., 3rd Revised ed.

Kumar, Shashi (2007). *Special Lecture Delivered in the Asian School of Journalism*, Chennai, India.

Lal, Sham (2003). *Indian Realities*, New Delhi : Rupa and Co.

Lasch, Christopher (2001). *The Culture of Narcissism: American Life in an Age of Diminishing Expectation*, New York : Norton.

Lasn, Kalle (1999). *Culture Jam: The Uncoiling of America*, New York : William Morrow and Company.

Lippmann, Walter (1922). *Public Opinion*, New York : Harcourt Brace, p. 268.

MacBride International Commissicn for the Study of Communication Problems (1980). Many Voices, One World, Report of the UNESCO, Paris.

Madhukar, R.K. (2001). *Business Communication and Customer Relations*, New Delhi : Vikas Publishing House Pvt. Ltd., pp. 1-18.

Manonmani, T. (1997). National Broadcasting Policy for Development, *Communicator*, XXXII (2): 19-22.

Marx, Karl and Friedrich Engels (1848). *Manifesto of the Communist Party*, p. 44.

Matsuda, Mari J. *et al.* (1993). Words that Wound: Critical Race Theory, Assaultive Speech and the First Amendment. Boulder, CO: Westview Press.

McChesney, Robert W. (2008). The Political Economy of Media: Enduring Issues, Emerging Dilemmas, *Monthly Review Press*, New York, pp. 132-249.

McQuail, Denis (1975). *Toward a Sociology of Communication*, London : Collier McMillian.

Menon, Vijay (1985). Information Flow in Asia—An Overview, *Media Asia*, 12 (2): 63-66.

Michael, V.P. (1996). *HRM and Human Relations*, Mumbai : Himalaya Publishing House, p. 32.

Miller and Rose (2009). *www.accessmylibrary.com*

Mohanty, Manashi and Pritishri Parhi (2002). Folk and Traditional Media: A Powerful Tool for Rural Development, College of Home Science, O.U.A.T., Bhubaneswar-751 003, Orissa, India, *E-mail:* manashiouat@gmail.com

Montagu, Ashley and Floyd Matson (2008). *The Human Connection*, New York : McGraw Hill.

Nair, Kiran Ramachandran (1997). Ethical Dilemmas and Social Responsibilities in Communication, *Communicator*, XXXII(2): 9-11.

Ninan, Sevanti (2007). *Headlines from the Heartland*, New Delhi : Sage Publications.

Nye, Joseph S. Jr. and William A. Owens (1996). America's Information Edge, *Foreign Affairs*, March/April: 20-36.

Panford, S., Nyaney, O.M., Grad Dip, Amoah, O.S., Aidoo, G.N. (2001). Using Folk Media in HIV/AIDS Prevention in Rural Ghana, *American Journal of Public Health*, 91 (10): 125-130.

Pavlik, J. and McIntosh (2005). *Media Convergence: New Possibilities and Opportunities*, p.71.

Piyadassi, Mahathera (1991). *The Spectrum of Buddhism, The Corporate Body of the Buddha Educational Foundation*, Taipei, Taiwan, R.O.C., pp. 403-415.

Prasad, Ravishankar (2002). Inaugural Address in the Two Day National Seminar an Media Policy, Organized by the Indian Institute of Mass Communication, New Delhi.

Rajagopal, Aravind (2001). *Politics after Television—Hindu Nationalism and the Reshaping of the Public in India*, Cambridge University Press, New York.

Ranganath, R. (2011). Status, Problems and Prospects of Corporate Advertising in Karnataka State: An Evaluation, unpublished Ph.D., Thesis, University of Mysore, India.

Robertson, R. (1995). Globalization: Time-Space and Homogeneity-Heterogeneity, In: Featherstone, M.L. and Robertson, R. eds., *Global Modernities*, CA, Thousand Oaks: Sage, p. 8.

Root, F.R. (1994). *Entry Strategies for International Markets*, San Fransisco: Jossey-Bass Inc. Publishers.

Rorty, James (1976). *Our Master's Voice: Advertising*, Chennai: Ayer Co. Pub.

Roy, Ash Narayan (1999). *Third World in the Age of Globalization*, New Delhi : Madhyam Books.

Sahai, Nandini (2002). Gender and Poverty—The Role of Media, *Communication Today*, 5(4): 6-16.

Sarabhai, Vikram and Chaudhury, Kamla (1974). *Television and Development, in Scientific Policy and National Development*, New Delhi : South Asian Books, Macmillan.

Schiller, Herbert (1985). *Information and the Crisis Economy*, Norwood, NJ: Ablex.

Shah, Kruti and Alan D'Souza (2009). *Advertising and Promotions: An IMC Perspective*, New Delhi : Tata McGraw-Hill, p. 642.

Signorielli, N. and Morgan, M. (Eds.) (1990). *Cultivation Analysis: New Directions in Media Effects Research*, Newbury Park: Sage.

Singh, Kavaljit (2005). *Questioning Globalization*, New Delhi : Madhyam Books.

Singhal, Arvind and Everett M. Rogers (2001). *India's Communication Revolution: From Bullock-Carts to Cyber-Marts*, New Delhi: Sage Publications.

Smith, Dennis (2006). *Globalization: The Hidden Agenda*, Cambridge: Polity, p. 1.

Sparks, Colin (2000). The Global, the Local and the Public Sphere. In Georgette Wang, Jan Servaes and Anura Goonasekera (Eds.), *The New Communications Landscape: Demystifying Media Globalization*, pp. 74-95. London: Routledge.

Straubhaar, J. and LaRose, R. (2004). *Media Now: Understanding Media, Culture, and Technology*. Thomson: Wadsworth, pp. 480-498.

Tehranian, Katharine and Majid Tehranian (1992). Restructuring for World Peace: On the Threshold of the 21st Century. Cresskill, N.J.: Hampton Press.

Tehranian, Majid (1977). *Communications Policy for National Development*, London: Routledge.

The Hindu (2007). Special Report, 130 (233): 19, July 17, Chennai, India.

Thoraval, Yves (2000). *The Cinemas of India*, New Delhi : MacMillan Publishers.

Toffler, Alvin (1992). *Power Shift: Knowledge, Wealth and Violence at the Edge of 21st Century*, New York : Bantam Books.

Tomlinson, J. (2002). The Discourse of Cultural Imperialism, In D. McQuail (Ed.), Mcquail's Reader in *Mass Communication Theory*, London: Sage Publications, pp. 223-237.

Ulrich, Dave (1998). 'Editor's Note', Human Resource Management, John Wiley and Sons Inc., Vol. 37 (3 and 4), p. 195

UNESCO (1978). *Declaration on Freedom of Expression*, Paris.

Veermani, Aravind (2000). A Communications Policy for the 21st Century, *Economic and Political Weekly,* 35(23): 1907-1910.

Vilanilam, J.V. (2005). *Mass Communication in India: A Sociological Perspective*, New Delhi : Sage Publications Ltd., p. 17.

Walker, Alexander (1984). *Foreword to 'Chronicle of Cinema'*, London : Allen Lane.

White, L.D. (1955). *Introduction to the Study of Public Administration*, New York: Crowwell Coller and MacMillan.

Wildman, S. and Siwek, S. (1988). *International Trade in Films and Television Program*, Cambridge, MA: Ballinger, pp. 136-37.

Wright, C.R. (1959). *Mass Communication: A Sociological Perspective*, New York: Random House, p. 21.

Young India, July 25, 1929.

Zwaal, P.N. (2000). Story Telling as a Vehicle for Improving Inter-Cultural Dialogue, Unpublished Thesis on Environmental Conservation in Cameroon.

Index